ITIL 4 FOUNDATION EXAM PREPARATION & PRACTICE TEST

BEGINNERS GUIDE FOR PASSING THE ITIL 4 EXAM FAST INCLUDING 50 TEST QUESTIONS

RICHIE MILLER

Disclaimer

Every effort was made to produce this book as truthful as possible, but no warranty is implied. The author shall have neither liability nor responsibility to any person or entity concerning any loss or damages ascending from the information contained in this book. The information in the following pages are broadly considered to be truthful and accurate of facts, and such any negligence, use or misuse of the information in question by the reader will render any resulting actions solely under their purview.

Table of Contents

Introduction

ITIL stands for Information Technology Infrastructure Library which is a widely adopted body of knowledge and best practices for successful IT Service Management that links with training and certification. ITIL 4 has evolved from the current version by re-shaping much of the established ITSM practices in the wider context of customer experience; value streams and digital transformation; as well as embracing new ways of working, such as Lean, Agile, and DevOps. ITIL certifications demonstrate that you are qualified in service Management best practices, utilizing processes, procedures, and methods that are common in modern IT. ITIL certified professionals are in high demand: they possess the skills to grow and transform the business. ITIL Foundation is the first ITIL 4 publication and the latest evolution of the most widely-adopted guidance for ITSM. Its audience ranges from IT and business students taking their first steps in service management to seasoned professionals familiar with earlier versions of ITIL and other sources of industry best practice. ITIL 4 provides the guidance organizations need to address new service management challenges and utilize the potential of modern technology. It is designed to ensure a flexible, coordinated and integrated system for the effective governance and management of IT-enabled services. The ITIL 4 Foundation certification is designed as an introduction to ITIL 4 and enables candidates to look at IT service management through an end-to-end operating model for the creation, delivery and continual improvement of tech-enabled products and services. This book offers 5 mock tests, including 50 Realistic ITIL Questions and answers with explanations to get you certified on your 1st attempt! Hence all you need to pass the ITIL 4 exam is this book! In fact, if you want to discover how to become an ITIL Professional, then let me share with you a brief summary of this book. First you will discover what is ITIL 4 Foundation and what are the 4 Dimensions of Service Management in ITIL. Next you will learn what is the ITIL 4 Service Value System and what are the elements of ITIL 4 Foundation framework. Moving on you will discover what are the General Management best practices, Service Management best practices and the Technical Management best practices. Net you will discover what is the difference between Change Management, Incident Management and Problem Management. After that, you will understand the ITIL 4 Foundation Guiding Principles, the ITIL 4 Foundation Continual Improvement as a Practice, the ITIL 4 Foundation Information Security Relationship and Supplier Management and the ITIL 4 Foundation IT Asset Monitoring & Event and Release Management best practices. Next, you will discover what is the difference between ITIL 4 Foundation Service Configuration and Deployment Management and ITIL versus IT Service Management. Moving on, you will discover how to implement the Change Management Process in 5 Steps and what are the best practices between Service Operations Management and ITSM. You will also discover what is the difference between Project Management and Service Management, what are the most common IT Operations Functions and what Interfaces within ITSM you should be aware of. Next you will discover what is the Value of ITSM Maintenance of IT Services, what are the Supplier Management Objectives and what is the difference between COBIT and ITIL. Lastly you will discover what is the Continual Improvement Model and what are the Benefits of Having an ITIL Certification. Finally, you will discover how to Prepare for ITIL 4 Foundation Exam Online and what are the 50 most common asked ITIL 4 Foundation Exam Questions, including all the answers and explanation so you can grasp a firm knowledge and pass your exam for the first attempt! As you see, this book is a comprehensive guide on ITIL4 Foundation and will reveal the must-have skills that every IT pro deploys daily. By finishing this book, you will become an IT professional, nevertheless, it is recommended to read the book or listen the audiobook several times to follow the provided guide. The audiobook listeners will receive a complementary PDF document, containing 50 mock exam questions and answers, hence it's also advantageous to highlight critical subjects to review them later using a paperback or hardcover book, or the accompanied PDF once printed out for your reference. If you are a complete beginner, having limited knowledge or no experience and want to speed up your ITIL skills, this book will provide a tremendous amount of value to you! If you already working in IT but you want to learn the latest tricks and tips, this book will be extremely useful to you. If you want to pass the ITIL 4 exam fast, let's first cover why ITIL is so important, what exactly it is, the history of ITIL, the types of ITIL versions and ITIL certificates!

Chapter 1 Introduction to ITIL 4 Foundation

ITIL is a set of detailed practices for IT Service Management that focuses on aligning IT Services for the needs of your business. Firstly we will talk about why ITIL is so important, what exactly it is, the history of ITIL, some of the advantages of ITIL, the types of ITIL versions and ITIL certificates. But why is ITIL so important? Let's understand this better by taking into consideration of a conversation. Imagine that we have two friends John and Jim talking to each other about ITIL. Jim asks how we can opt for a holistic approach in the IT industry? By this he means that instead of taking each of the components in the IT industry separately, how can he take them as a whole or how can we see it as a whole? That's when John says that earlier it was difficult but now it isn't. All of that was possible with the help of ITIL. With IT, businesses could collaborate with the IT team so that they could deliver IT Services to the stakeholders. Jim is really interested and wants to know more about the benefits of ITIL. Some of the benefits of ITIL are reduced IT costs, enhanced IT Services, improved productivity, improved return on investment, improved customer satisfaction, better Management of business risk and service disruption and improved resource utilization. But first we're going to talk about what exactly ITIL is. ITIL stands for Information Technology Infrastructure Library. It helps all organizations to deliver IT Services using the most efficient methods. It helps businesses to improve service levels and reduce the cost of IT Operations. But service levels has a different meaning. It basically focuses on how an organization maintains IT Services for customers as well as it controls various activities involved in the process, activities like planning designing delivering deploying and managing services. The main goal of ITIL is to improve efficiency and achieve predictable service delivery. At the same time a major requirement is to achieve high service quality. Now let's talk about the history of ITIL. ITIL first was introduced in 1989 to standardize IT Service Management. To provide for a uniform structure for service delivery, ITIL second version was introduced in 2001. In 2007 ITIL third version was introduced. This has aimed to improve ITIL Service lifecycle by introducing a new feature of feedback looping. Aiming to clarify the processes of ideas third version a new version of ITIL v3 was upgraded and released in 2011. In 2019 ITIL's fourth version was introduced. It provided a flexible as well as integrity system for the effective Management of IT enabled services. Now let's talk about the benefits of ITIL. ITIL provides greater reliability, it improves the decision-making process, you have a greater return on investment, the quality of service is much better and it's also cost efficient. Now let's talk about the different types of ITIL. ITIL has five revisions. ITIL v1 to v4. ITIL v1 talks about processes that are involved in service support such as helpdesk Management, Change Management and software distribution. Organizations and government agencies around the world began adopting the framework in the early 90s to improve their IT Services and delivery capabilities. The first version consists of four major concepts; availability Management, capacity Management, contingency Management and cost Management. First let's talk about availability Management. We all know that in an organization there are several IT Services. These could include infrastructure, processes, roles and much more. Availability Management ensures that these are available based on the business requirement. Next we have capacity Management. If there are any performance based issues beaten services or resources, its handled by capacity Management. Next we have contingency Management. With this you're able to identify vulnerabilities and make sure that such Incidents don't happen again. And finally we have cost Management. With this you are able to deliver as well as manage cost effective idea assets and resources. Next let's have a look at the second version of ITIL - ITIL v2. This version of ITIL was published in the year 2001. It focused on the removal of duplicate entries helped improve the consistency of topics and inclusion of new IT concepts. Some of the topics that were covered in idea to a Problem Management, release Management, Incident Management and much more. ITIL v2 consists of two major concepts. The first one is service support. With this you're delivered processors so that you can control service interruptions. Now let's talk about service delivery. This provides a set of principles, policies as well as constraints which can be utilized for designing, building and deploying services that are delivered by service providers. One thing you should keep in mind is that the second version of ITIL did not have an organized service lifecycle unlike the version three that we got to talk about very soon. Version 3 of ITIL was published in 2007 and it adopted more of a lifecycle approach to Service Management with a greater emphasis on IT business integration. This is another upgrade and consists of 26 processes and functions and that this version consists of five major sections. Let's have a look at each of these sections. Firstly we have service strategy, service design, service transition, service Operations and continual service improvement. First off let's have a look at service strategy. This is the process where you understand what the clients requirements are. What is the client want from your business. Secondly we have service design. This aims so that you can design IT Services in an effective as well as efficient manner. In the third step we have service transition. With this you can plan, build, test and deploy the services into the customers environments. Our fourth step involves service Operations now this maintains this ensures that access to IT Services is only given to authorized users and the issue of service failure is minimized. Finally we have a continual service improvement. This makes sure that the IT Services are always aligned to the business's needs. Now let's have a look at the 2011 update of

ITIL Version three. This edition of ITIL is an improvement over the previous edition. It aimed to resolve the mistakes as well as inconsistencies in the text and diagrams across the suite. This version underwent a lot of redesigning and use of a larger font intended to make ITIL a little more approachable to the reader. This version majorly highlights the service strategy volume. This version doesn't have a lot of changes but has a few important update. Firstly let's have a look at service strategy. In this version a new service called service strategy Manager was introduced. This was for people who created as well as implemented IT strategies that aligned with the business requirements. Secondly we have service design. This implemented technical standards to the service design process as well as coordinated all the activities across all designs. Next we have service transition. This introduced something known as effective Change Management which minimized the chances of service failure. For the fourth major concept we have service Operations. The latest update of service operation provides as well as maintains the processes for effective and efficient handling of Service Requests. Finally we have continual service improvement. With the clear and concise seven step model you're introduced to the improvement process. These seven steps are identifying the strategy for improvement, defining what exactly you will measure, gathering the data, processing the data, analyzing this Information, presenting and using the Information and implementing improvement. And now where is the current version of ITIL – ITILv4. The main goal of ITIL v4 is to help all organizations deliver IT Services using the most effective methods. ITIL can be utilized with the number of different frameworks such as Agile, Lean and DevOps. ITIL 4 consists of two major components. The four dimensions model and the ITIL service value system. Now let's have a look at the four dimensions model. Firstly we have organizations and people. People in the organization need to understand what the roles and responsibilities are. They need to have a clear understanding of how their role adds value to the organization. Then we have Information and Technology. This includes Information, knowledge, techniques and technologies that are required for Service Management. Next we have partners and suppliers. This basically sets up contracts and other agreements between the organization and their partners. Here there's a focus on the organization's relationship with businesses like the ones that are involved in design, deployment, delivery, support and the continual improvement of services. Finally we have value streams and processes. A value stream is basically a series of steps that an organization follows so they can create as well as deliver products or services to a consumer. A well-defined process can greatly improve productivity within or across organizations. It's very important that an organization addresses all of these four different dimensions to ensure that high service quality is maintained. Now let's have a look at the service value system. This is a set of activities that are performed by an organization so that they deliver a valuable output to the end users or consumers. The SVS includes elements such as guiding principles, governance, service value chain, continual improvement and practices. First let's have a look at guiding principles. These are a set of principles that help in providing a comprehensive understanding of a series of steps of how an organization should manage a service. Secondly we have governance; and this is responsible for controlling as well as monitoring the organization. It can adapt to the guiding principles or it can define its own set of principles. Next we have service value chain. This is a set of activities that the business performs so that they can provide a valuable product or service to its consumers. Next, we have continual improvement. This ensures that IT Services are continuously aligned to the customers expectations. Finally we have Management practices. These are 34 Management practices that are designed so that an organization is able to achieve its goals. These practices are divided into three major categories.

Firstly we have general Management practices, Service Management practices and technical Management practices. Now let's talk about ITIL Certifications. It's not only necessary that you learn about ITIL but it's very important that you get certified in it. ITIL has its own Certifications. Firstly we have the Foundation Certification which is an entry level Certification and it includes all the concepts of ITIL Service lifecycle and Service Management practices. After which you can take the next level exam which is the Practitioner Certification. This is a higher level examination which aims to increase the ability of the individual who's writing the test to adopt and adapt ITIL to their organization. Then we have the Intermediate Certification which helps an individual understand how to manage and coordinate the ITIL practice areas. One thing you should note is that if you are preparing for the Certification, you need to have a minimum of two years of experience in IT Service Management. Next we have the Expert Level Certification which covers the depth of ITIL processes and practices across all ITIL disciplines. Now for the final level, which is the master level Certification. Here an individual is able to explain advanced methods of ITIL techniques and Management practices. To achieve this Certification, you need to have a minimum of two years of experience in the IT Service Management.

Chapter 2 4 Dimensions of Service Management in ITIL

By the end of this chapter you will be able to list the four dimensions of Service Management, describe the factors that influence an organization strategy and outline the benefits of value streams and processes. Let's look at the dimensions of Service Management. To support a holistic approach to Service Management ITIL defines four dimensions of Service Management that collectively are critical to the effective and efficient facilitation of value for customers and other stakeholders in the form of products and services. These are organizations and people, Information and Technology, partners and suppliers, value streams and processes. None of these are sufficient to produce the required outcome when considered in isolation. These four dimensions represent perspective which are relevant to the whole service value system or SVS and all IT Services being managed, including the entirety of the service value chain and all practices. The four dimensions are constrained or influenced by several external factors that are often beyond the control of the SVS. Failing to address all four dimensions properly may result in services becoming undeliverable or not meeting expectations of quality or efficiency. The four dimensions do not have sharp boundaries and may overlap. They will sometimes interact in unpredictable ways, depending on the level of complexity and uncertainty in which an organization operates. Now let's look at the organizations and people. The first dimension of Service Management is organizations and people. The organization and people dimension of a Service covers roles and responsibilities, formal organizational structures, culture and required staffing and competencies - all of which are related to the creation delivery and improvement of a service. When looking at this dimension in relation to the SVS the focus should be on the same aspects but in the context of the organization acting as a service provider. The complexity of organizations is growing and it is important to ensure that the way an organization is structured and managed as well as its roles, responsibilities and systems of authority and communication is well-defined and supports its overall strategy and operating model. The organization also needs a culture that supports its objectives and the right level of capacity and competency among its workforce. The effectiveness of an organization cannot be assured by a formally established structure or system of authority alone. It is vital that the leaders of the organization champion and advocate values which motivate people to work in desirable ways. Ultimately however it is the way in which an organization carries out its work that creates shared values and attitudes which over time are considered to be the organization's culture. It is useful to promote a culture of trust and transparency in an organization that encourages its members to raise and escalate issues and facilitate communication before any issues have an impact on customers. Adopting the ITIL guiding principles can be a good starting point for establishing a healthy organizational culture. Be it customers employees of suppliers employees of the service provider or any other stakeholder in the service relationship are a key element in this dimension. Organizations need people who pay attention not only to the skills and competencies of teams or individual members but also to Management and leadership styles. Have good communication and collaboration skills, update their skills and competencies over a period of time, understand the interfaces but they're specializations and roles and those of others in the organization, have proper levels of collaboration and coordination among people, have a broad general knowledge of the other areas of the organization, combined with a deep specialization in certain fields. Let's move on to the next dimension; Information and Technology. The second dimension of Service Management is Information and Technology. As with the other three dimensions, Information and Technology applies both the Service Management and to the services being managed. When applied to the service value system, the Information and Technology dimension includes the Information and knowledge necessary for the Management of services, as well as the technologies required. It also incorporates the relationships between different components of the SVS such as the inputs and outputs of activities and practices. The technologies that support Service Management include but are not limited to workflow Management systems, knowledge bases, inventory systems, communication systems and analytical tools. Service Management increasingly benefits from Technology development with newer technologies such as artificial intelligence, machine learning and other cognitive computing solutions. They are used at all levels, from a strategic planning and portfolio optimization to system monitoring and user support. The use of mobile platforms, cloud solutions, remote collaboration tools, automated testing and deployment solutions has become a common practice among service providers. In the context of a specific IP service this dimension includes the Information created, managed and used in the course of service provision and consumption and the technologies that support and enable that service. The specific Information and technologies depend on the nature of the services being provided and usually cover all levels of IT architecture including applications, databases, communication systems and their integrations. In many areas, IT Services utilize the latest Technology developments such as blockchain, artificial intelligence and cognitive computing. These services provide a business differentiation potential to early adopters especially in highly competitive industries. Other Technology solutions such as cloud computing or mobile apps have become a common practice across many industries globally. For many services, Information Management is the primary means of delivering customer value. Information is generally the key output of the majority of IT Services which are consumed by business customers. Another key consideration in this dimension is the way Information is exchanged between different services and service components. The Information architecture of various services should be well understood and continually optimized, considering such criteria as the availability, reliability, accessibility, timeliness, accuracy and relevance of the Information provided to users and exchanged between services. The challenges of Information Management such as those presented by security and regulatory compliance requirements are also a focus of this dimension. Let's now look at some of the regulations the Information and Technology. Organization must consider how Information is exchanged between different services and service components. For example an organization may be subject to the European Union's general data protection regulation or GDPR which influences its Information Management policies and practices. Other industries or countries may have regulations that impose constraints on the collection and Management of data of multinational corporations. For example in the United States the Health Insurance Portability and Accountability Act of 1996 provides data privacy and security provisions for safeguarding medical Information collected in the US. Let's look at how to select the right Technology. Most services nowadays are based on Information Technology and are heavily dependent on it. When considering a Technology for use in the planning, design, transition or operation of a product or service, questions that an organization can ask may include the following. Is this Technology compatible with the current architecture of the organization and its customers? Does this Technology raise any regulatory or other compliance issues with the organization's policies and Information security controls or those of its customers? Is this a Technology that will continue to be viable in the foreseeable future? Is the organization willing to accept the risk of using aging Technology or of embracing emerging or unproven Technology? Does this Technology align with the strategy of the service provider or its service consumers, does the organization have the right skills across its staff and suppliers to support and maintain the Technology? Does this Technology have sufficient automation capabilities to ensure it can be efficiently developed, deployed and operated? Does this Technology offer additional capabilities that might be leveraged for other products or services? Does this Technology introduce new risks or constraints to the organization? Let's look at the factors influencing Technology. The culture of an organization may have a significant impact on the technologies it chooses to use. Some organizations will have more of an interest in being on the cutting edge of technological advances than others. Equally, the culture of some organizations may be focused on a more traditional way of working. One company may be excited to take advantage of artificial intelligence technologies, while another may barely be ready for advanced data analysis tools. The nature of the business will also affect the Technology it makes use of. For example a company that does significant business with government clients may have restrictions on the use of some technologies or have significantly higher security concerns that must be addressed. Other industries such as finance or life sciences are also subject to restrictions around their use of Technology. For example they usually cannot use open source and public services when dealing with sensitive data. Let's now move on to our next topic; cloud computing. Cloud computing is a model for enabling on-demand network access to a shared pool of configurable computing resources that can be rapidly provided with minimal Management effort or provider interaction. ITSM has been focusing on value for users and customers for years and this focus is usually Technology agnostic. What matters is not the Technology but the opportunities it creates for the customers. Although for the most part this is a perfectly acceptable approach, organizations cannot ignore new architectural solutions and the evolution of Technology in general. Cloud computing has become an architectural shift in IT, introducing new opportunities and risks and organizations have reacted to it in ways that are most beneficial for themselves, their customers and other stakeholders. Key characteristics of cloud computing include on-demand availability, often self-service, network access, often internet access, resource pooling, often among multiple organizations, rapid elasticity, often automatic, and measured service, often from service consumers perspective. Now let's learn about partners and suppliers. The third dimension of Service Management is partners and suppliers. Every organization and service depends on services provided by other organisations to some extent. The partners and suppliers dimension encompasses an organization's relationships with other organisations that are involved in the design, development, deployment, delivery, support and continual improvement of services. It also incorporates contracts and other agreements between the organization and its partners or suppliers. A method and organization may use to address the partners and suppliers dimension is service integration and Management. This involves the use of a specially established integrator to ensure that service relationships are properly coordinated. Service integration and Management may be kept within the organization, but can also be delegated to a trusted partner. Relationships between organisations may involve various levels of integration and formality. This ranges from formal contracts with clear separation of responsibilities to flexible partnerships where parties share common goals and risks and collaborate to achieve desired outcomes. Note that the forms of cooperation described in the given table are not fixed and distinctive but exist as a scale.

Form of cooperation	Outputs	Responsibility for the outputs	Responsibility for achievement of the outcomes	Level of formality	Examples
Goods supply	Goods supplied	Supplier	Customer	Formal supply contract or invoices	Procurement of computers and phones
Service delivery	Services delivered	Provider	Customer	Formal agreements and flexible cases	Cloud computing (infrastructure of platform as a service)
Service partnership	Value co-created	Shared between provider and customer	Shared between provider and customer	Shared goals, generic agreements, flexible case-based arrangements	Employee onboarding (shared between HR, facilities, and IT)

An organization acting as a service provider will have a position on this scale, which will vary depending on the strategy and objectives for customer relationships. Likewise when an organization acts as a service consumer, the role it takes on will depend on its strategy and objectives for sourcing and supplier Management. Now let's look at organization strategy. An organization strategy when it comes to choosing partners and suppliers should be based on its goals, culture and business environment. For example some organizations may believe that they will be best served by focusing their attention on developing certain core competencies, using partners and suppliers to provide other needs. Other organizations may choose to rely as much as possible on their own resources using partners and suppliers as little as possible. There are of course many variations between these two opposite approaches. Factors that may influence an organization strategy when using suppliers include strategic focus.

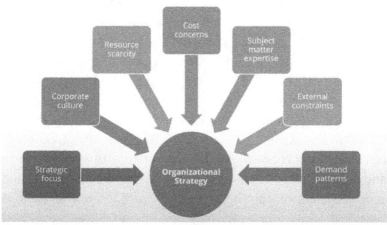

Some organizations may prefer to focus on their core competence and to outsource non core supporting functions to third parties. Others may prefer to stay as self-sufficient as possible, retaining full control over all important functions. Corporate culture; some organizations have a historical preference for one approach over another. Long-standing cultural bias is difficult to change without compelling reasons. Resource scarcity; if a required resource or skill set is in short supply, it may be difficult for the service provider to acquire what is needed without engaging a supplier. Cost concerns; a decision may be influenced by the service providers belief that it can source a particular requirement more economically from a supplier. Subject matter expertise; the service provider may believe that it is less risky to use a supplier that already has expertise in a required area, rather than trying to develop and maintain the subject-matter expertise in-house. External constraints; government regulation or policy, industry codes of conduct and social political or legal constraints might impact an organization's supplier strategy. Demand patterns; customer activity or demand for services might be seasonal or demonstrate high degrees of variability. These patterns may impact the extent to which organizations use external service providers to cope with variable demand.

Let's now look at value streams and processes. The fourth dimension of Service Management is value streams and processes. Like the other dimensions, this dimension is applicable to both the service value systems in general and to specific products and services. In both contexts, it defines the activities, workflows, controls and procedures needed to achieve the agreed objectives. Applied to the organization and its service value systems, the value streams and processes dimension is concerned with how the various parts of the organization work in an integrated and coordinated way to enable value creation through products and services. It also focuses on what activities the organization undertakes, how they are organized, as well as how the organization ensures that it is enabling value creation for all stakeholders efficiently and effectively. A value stream is a series of steps that an organization uses to create and deliver products and services to a service consumer. A value stream is a combination of the organization's value chain activities.

Benefits of value streams

Identifying and understanding the various value streams that an organization has is critical to improving its overall performance. Value stream helps to have a clear picture of what it delivers and how and to make continual improvements to its services. Organizations can map their work with the identified value stream map. This would enable them to analyze their current state and identify any barriers to workflow and non value-adding activities, for example waste. Opportunities to increase value adding activities can be found across the service value chain. These may be new activities or modifications to existing ones which can make the organization more productive. Value stream optimization may include process automation or adopting of emerging technologies and ways of work to gain efficiencies or enhance user experience. Depending on the organization strategy, value streams can be redefined to react to changing demand and other circumstances or remain stable for a significant amount of time.

A process is a set of interrelated or interacting activities that transform inputs into outputs. Processes define the sequence of activities and their dependencies. Processes describe what needs to be done in order to accomplish an objective and a well-defined process can improve productivity within and across organizations. They are usually detailed in procedures which outline who is involved in the process and work instructions which explain how they are carried out. An organization should answer the following questions to successfully create, deliver and improve a service. What is the generic delivery model for the service and how does the service work? What are the value streams involved in delivering the agreed outputs of the service? Who or what performs the required service actions? Specific answers to these questions will vary depending on the nature and architecture of the service. Let's now look at some of the factors that affect service providers. Service providers do not operate in isolation. They are affected by many external factors and work in dynamic and complex environments that can exhibit high degrees of volatility and uncertainty and impose constraints on how the service provider can work. In order to analyze these external factors, frameworks such as the pestle model are used. Pestle is an acronym for political, economic, social, technological, legal and environmental which represent the factors that constrain or influence how a service provider operates. Collectively, these factors influence how organizations configure their resources and address the four dimensions of Service Management. Political factors include laws, regulations, policies, bureaucracy, corruption, trade unions and import or export restrictions. Political factors can also compromise laws around data protection, consumer protection, copyright, patent and intellectual property. Economic factors include consumer income and disposable income, monetary and fiscal policies especially in countries where the government has limited involvement in central bank functions, stock market trends, interest rates economic growth and labor costs. Social factors include consumer lifestyles and buying habits, attitudes and expectations of product and service quality and social makeup. For example family size or structure, social classes or age distribution. Technological factors include considerations around available private and public infrastructure from roads and public utilities to communications infrastructure. Rate of Technology change, level of Technology adoption especially in the context of the organization's industry and competition, internet penetration and adoption of smartphones. Legal factors include laws around antitrust, copyright, consumer protection, employment, Health and Safety and data protection. Environmental factors include whether, climate change, pollution and laws designed to regulate or tackle pollution and waste Management, attitudes from businesses and consumers toward renewable energy and environmentally friendly products and services.

Here are the key takeaways. The four dimensions of Service Management are organizations and people, Information and Technology, partners and suppliers and value streams and processes. The Information and Technology dimension includes the Information and knowledge necessary for the Management of services and the technologies required. The partners and suppliers dimension encompasses an organization's relationships with other organizations that are involved in the design, development, deployment, delivery, support and continual improvement of services. Services are affected by many external factors that exhibit high degrees of volatility and uncertainty and the pose constraints on how they work.

Chapter 3 ITIL 4 Service Value System

By the end of this chapter, you will be able to describe the ITIL service value system, describe the nature use and interaction of the guiding principles and explain the use of the guiding principles. The ITIL SVS describes how all the components and activities of the organization work together as a system to enable value creation. Each organization's SVS has interfaces with other organizations. This creates an ecosystem that facilitates value for those organizations, their customers and other stakeholders. SVS ensures that the organization continually Co creates value with all stakeholders through the use and Management of products and services. These components and activities together with the organization's resources can be configured and reconfigured in multiple combinations in a flexible way as circumstances change, but this requires the integration and coordination of activities, practices, teams, authorities and responsibilities of all parties to be truly effective. The key inputs to the SVS are opportunity and demand. Opportunities represent options or possibilities to add value for stakeholders or otherwise improve the organization. Demand is the need or desire for products and services among internal and external consumers. The outcome of the SVS is value - the perceived benefits usefulness and importance of something. The ITIL SVS can enable the creation of many different types of value for a wide group of stakeholders. Opportunity and demand trigger activities within the ITIL SVS and these activities lead to the creation of value, however the organization does not automatically accept all opportunities or satisfy all demand. There may not be demand for these opportunities yet, but they can still trigger work within the system. Organizations should prioritize new or changed services with opportunities for improvement to ensure their resources are correctly allocated. The ITIL SVS includes the following components; guiding principles, recommendations that can guide an organization in all circumstances regardless of changes in its goals, strategies, type of work or Management structure, governance - the means by which an organization is directed and controlled, service value chain - a set of interconnected activities that an organization performs to deliver a valuable product or service to its consumers and to facilitate value realization, practices - set of organizational resources designed for performing work or accomplishing an objective, continual improvement - a recurring organizational activity performed at all levels to ensure that an organization's performance continually meets stakeholders expectations. ITIL 4 supports continual improvement with the ITIL continual improvement model. One of the biggest challenges an organization can face when trying to work effectively and efficiently with the shared vision or to become more Agile and resilient is the presence of organizational silos. Organizational silos can form in many ways and for many different reasons. Silos can be resistant to change and can prevent easy access to the Information and specialized expertise that exists across the organization, which can in turn reduce efficiency and increase both cost and risk. Silos also make it more difficult for communication or collaboration to occur across different groups. A siloed organization cannot act quickly to take advantage of opportunities or to optimize the utilization of resources across the organization. It is often unable to make effective decisions about changes due to limited visibility and many hidden agendas. Practices can also become silos. Many organizations have implemented practices like Change Management or Incident Management without clear interfaces with other practices. The ITIL SVS has been specifically architected to enable flexibility and discourage siloed working. The service value chain activities and the practices in the SVS do not form a fixed rigid structure, rather they can be combined in multiple value streams to address the needs of the organization in a variety of scenarios. Organizations should be able to define and redefine their value streams in a flexible yet safe and efficient manner. This requires continual improvement activity to be carried out at all levels of the organization. The ITIL continual improvement model helps to structure this activity. Finally, the continual improvement and overall operation of an organization are shaped by the ITIL guiding principles. The guiding principles create a Foundation for a shared culture across the organization, thus supporting collaboration and cooperation within and between the teams and removing the need for constraints and controls previously provided by silos. With these components the ITIL SVS supports many work approaches such as Agile, DevOps and Lean as well as traditional processes and Project Management with a flexible value oriented operating model. A guiding principle is a recommendation that guides an organization in all circumstances, regardless of changes in its goals, strategies, type of work or Management structure. A guiding principle is Universal and enduring. Guiding principles can be used to guide organizations in their work as they adopt the Service Management approach and adapt ITIL guidance to their own specific needs and circumstances. These principles are also reflected in many other frameworks, methods, standards, philosophies and/or bodies of knowledge such as Lean, Agile, DevOps and COBIT. These principles allow organizations to effectively integrate the use of multiple methods into an overall approach to Service Management. The guiding principles are universally applicable to nearly any initiative and to relationships with all stakeholder groups. The guiding principles encourage and support organizations and continual improvement at all levels. Let's review a high-level introduction to the guiding principles. Focus on value, start where you are, progress iteratively with feedback, collaborate and promote visibility, think and work holistically, keep it simple and practical and optimize and automate.

Focus on value

Everything the organization does should directly or indirectly create value for itself, its customers and other stakeholders. It is mostly focused on the creation of value for service consumers, however a service also contributes value for the organization and other stakeholders. The following recommendations can be adapted to address various stakeholder groups and the value that is created for them by the organization. Who is the service consumer? When focusing on value the first step is to know who is being served. In each situation the service provider must determine who the service consumer is and who the key stakeholders are. The consumers perspective of value; the service provider must understand what is truly a value to the service consumer. The service provider needs to know why the consumer uses the services, what the service has helped them to do, how the services help consumers achieve their goals, the role of cost or financial consequences for the service consumer and the risk involved for the service consumer.

Value for the service consumer

Is defined by the consumers needs? Is achieved through the support of intended outcomes and optimization of the service consumers costs and risks? Changes over time and in different circumstances? The customer experience or CX may also be called a user experience or UX is an important element of value. CX can be seen as the entirety of the interactions a customer has with the organization and its products or services. This experience can determine how the customer feels about the organization and its products and services. CX can be both objective and subjective. Let's look at how to apply the principle focus on value. To apply this principle successfully, consider this advice. Know how service consumers use each service, understand their expected outcomes, how each service contributes to these and how the service consumers perceive the service provider, collect feedback on a value on an ongoing basis and not just at the beginning of the service relationship, encourage a focus on value among all staff, teach staff to have to be aware of who their customers are and to understand CX, focus on value during normal operational activity as well as during improvement initiatives. The organization as a whole contributes to the value that the customer perceives and so everybody within the organization must maximize the value they create. The creation of value should not be left only to the people working on exciting projects and new things. Include focus on value in every step of any improvement initiative. Everybody involved in an improvement initiative needs to understand what outcomes the initiative is trying to facilitate, how its value will be measured and how they should be contributing to the co-creation of that value. Let's look at the second guiding principle; start where you are. What engaged in any improvement initiative do not start over without first considering what is already available to be leveraged. Starting without considering the past could be extremely wasteful in terms of time and loss of existing services, processes, people and tools that could have a significant value in the improvement effort. Decisions on how to proceed should be based on Information that is as accurate as possible. Services and methods already in place should be measured and/or observed directly to properly understand their current state and what can be reused from them. Decisions on how to proceed should be based on Information that is as accurate as possible. Within organizations, there is frequently a discrepancy between reports and reality. This is due to the difficulty of accurately measuring certain data or the unintentional bias or distortion of data that is produced through reports. Getting data from the source helps to avoid assumptions which if proven to be unfounded can be disastrous to timelines, budgets and the quality of results. Good hearts law states that when a measure becomes a target it ceases to be a good measure. The use of measurement is important to this principle. It should however be used to support the analysis of what has been observed, rather than to replace it as over reliance on data analytics and reporting can unintentionally introduce biases and risks in decision-making. For example if a Service Desk focuses on length of time spent on the phone, in addition it might also focus on minimizing the negative impact to customers or users, thus leading to a good user experience, which results in enabling users to resume their work. Metrics need to be meaningful and should directly relate to the desired outcome. Let's look at how to apply the principle, start where you are. Look at what exists as objectively as possible using the customer or the desired outcome as the starting point are the elements of the current state fit for purpose and fit for use. There are likely to be many elements of the current services, practices, projects and skills that can be used to create the desired future state provided the people making this judgment are objective. When examples of successful practices or services are found in the current state, determine if and how these can be replicated or expanded upon to achieve the desired state. In many if not most cases, leveraging what already exists will reduce the amount of work needed to transition from the current state to the desired state. Apply your Risk Management skills. There are risks associated with reusing existing practices and processes. There are also risk associated with putting something new in place. These should be considered as part of the decision-making process and the risks of making or not making a change could be evaluated to decide on the best course of action. Recognize that sometimes nothing from the current state can be reused, regardless of how desirable it may be to reuse, repurpose and recycle or even upcycle, there will be times when the only way to achieve the desired result is to start over entirely. Let's learn about the third guiding principle; progressed iteratively with feedback. Improvement iterations can be sequential or simultaneous based on the requirements of the improvement and what resources are available. Each individual iteration should be both manageable and managed, ensuring that tangible results are returned in a timely manner and built upon to create further improvement. When the iteration is being undertaken, circumstances can change and new priorities can arise and the need for the iteration may be altered or even eliminated. Seeking and using feedback before throughout and after each iteration will ensure that actions are focused and appropriate, even in changing circumstances. A feedback loop is a term commonly used to refer to a situation where part of the output of an activity is used for a new input. In a well-functioning organization, feedback is actively collected and processed along the value chain. Well-constructed feedback mechanisms facilitate the understanding of end user and customer perception of the value created, the efficiency and effectiveness of value chain activities, the effectiveness of service governance as well as Management controls, the interfaces between the organization and its partner and supplier network, the demand for products and services. Once received, feedback can be analyzed to identify improvement opportunities risks and issues. Working in a time-boxed iterative manner with feedback loops embedded into the process allows for greater flexibility, faster responses to customers and business needs, the ability to discover and respond to failure earlier and an overall improvement in quality. Let's see how to apply the principle progress iteratively with feedback. To apply this principle successfully, consider this advice. Comprehend the whole but do something. Understanding the big picture is important but so is making progress. The greatest enemy to progressing iteratively can be the desire to understand and account for everything. Analysis, paralysis - so much time is spent analyzing the situation that nothing ever gets done about it. The ecosystem is constantly changing so feedback is essential. Use feedback at all times and at all levels. Fast does not mean in complete - just because an iteration is small enough to be done quickly, does not mean it should not include all the elements necessary for success. Use minimal Viable Product - a version of the final product which allows the maximum amount of validated learning with the least effort. Let's move on to our next guiding principle; collaborate and promote visibility. When initiatives involve the right people in the correct roles, efforts benefit from better buy-in, more relevance because better Information is available for decision-making and increased likelihood of long-term success. Recognition of the need for genuine collaboration has been one of the driving factors in the evolution of what is now known as DevOps. Without effective collaboration neither Agile, Lean nor any other ITSM framework or method will work. Identifying and managing all the stakeholder groups that an organization deals with is important as the people and perspectives necessary for successful collaboration can be sourced within these stakeholder groups. A stakeholder is anyone who has a stake in the activities of the organization, including the organization itself, its customers or users and many others. Stakeholder collaboration include developers working with other internal teams to ensure that what is being developed can be operated efficiently and effectively, relationship Managers collaborating with service consumers to achieve a comprehensive understanding of service consumer needs and priorities, customers collaborating with each other to create a shared understanding of their business issues, internal and external suppliers collaborating with each other to review shared processes and identify opportunities for optimization and potential automation. Insufficient visibility of work leads to poor decision-making which in turn impacts the organization's ability to improve internal capabilities. It will then become difficult to drive improvements as it will not be clear which ones are likely to have the greatest positive impact on results. To avoid this, the organization needs to perform such critical analysis activities as understanding the flow of work in progress, identifying bottlenecks as well as excess capacity and uncovering waste. Let's now learn how to apply the principle collaborate and promote visibility. To apply this principle successfully consider this advice. Collaboration does not mean consensus - it is not necessary or even always wise to get consensus from everyone involved before proceeding. Some organizations are so concerned with getting consensus that they try to make everyone happy and end up either doing nothing or producing something that does not properly suit anyone's needs. Communicate in a way the audience can hear, selecting the right method and message for each audience is critical for success. The same traditional method for all communication will not work. Decisions can only be made on visible data. Making decisions in the absence of data is risky. Decisions should be made about what data is needed and therefore what work needs to be made visible. There may be a cost to collecting data and the organization must balance that cost against the benefit and intended usage of the data. Let's now move to the fifth principle; think and work holistically. Taking a holistic approach to Service Management includes establishing an understanding of how all the parts of an organization work together in an integrated way. It requires into invisibility of how demand is captured and translated into outcomes. In a complex system, the alteration of one element can impact others and where possible these impacts need to be identified, analyzed and planned for. Let's learn about applying the principle think and work holistically. To apply this principle successfully consider this advice. Recognize the complexity of the system's. Different levels of complexity require different heuristics for decision making. Applying methods and rules designed for a simple system can be ineffective or even harmful in a complex system where relationships between components are complicated and change more frequently. Collaboration is the key to thinking and working holistically. If the right mechanisms are put in place for all relevant stakeholders to collaborate in a timely manner, it will be possible to address any issue holistically without being unduly delayed. Where possible, look for patterns in the need of and interactions between system elements. Draw a knowledge in each area to identify what is essential for success and which relationships between elements influence the outcomes. With this Information, needs can be anticipated, standards can be set and a holistic viewpoint can be achieved. Automation can facilitate working holistically. Where the opportunity and sufficient resources are available automation can support end-to-end visibility for the organization and provide an efficient means of integrated Management. The sixth principle is keep it simple and practical. Outcome based thinking should be used to produce practical solutions that deliver valuable outcomes. Always use the minimum number of steps to accomplish an objective. When analyzing a practice, process, service metric or other improvement target always ask whether it contributes to value creation. When designing or improving Service

Management, it is better to start with an uncomplicated approach and then carefully add controls, activities or metrics when it is seen that they are truly needed. When designing managing or operating practices be mindful of conflicting objectives. Let's see how to apply the principle; keep it simple and practical. Every activity should contribute to the creation of value. Simplicity is the ultimate sophistication. It may seem harder to simplify but it is often more effective. Do fewer things but do them better. Minimizing activities to include only those with value for one or more stakeholders will allow for more focus on the quality of those actions. Respect the time of the people involved. A process that is too complicated and bureaucratic is a poor use of the time of the people involved. Easier to understand, more likely to adopt. To embrace a practice, make sure it is easy to follow. When improving daily Operations activities, quick wins allow organizations to demonstrate progress and manage stakeholder expectations. Working in an iterative way with feedback will quickly deliver incremental value at regular intervals. Let's look at the last principle; optimize and automate. Optimization means to make something as effective and useful as it needs to be. Before an activity can be effectively automated, it should be optimized to whatever degree is possible and reasonable. Regardless of the specific techniques, the path to optimization follows these high-level steps; understand and agree to the context in which the proposed optimization exists, the overall vision and objectives of the organization, assess the current state of the proposed optimization where it can be approved and which improvement opportunities are likely to produce the biggest positive impact. Agree what the future state and priorities of the organization should be, focusing on simplification and value, standardization of practices and services. Ensure the optimization has the appropriate level of stakeholder engagement and commitment. Execute the improvements in an iterative way. Continually monitor the impact of optimization. This will help to identify opportunities to improve methods of working. Automation typically refers to the use of Technology to perform a step or series of steps correctly and consistently with limited or no human intervention. For example automating frequent and repetitive tasks helps organizations scale up and allows human resources to be used for more complex decision-making. In its simplest form however, automation could also mean the standardization and streamlining of manual tasks such as defining the rules of part of a process to allow decisions to be made automatically. Efficiency can be greatly increased by reducing the need for human involvement to stop and evaluate each part of a process. Let's now look at how to apply the principle optimize and automate. Simplify and/or optimized before automating. Attempting to automate something that is complex or suboptimal will not be likely to achieve the desired outcome. Take time to map out the standard and repeating processes as far as possible and streamline where you can optimize. From there you can start to automate. Define your metrics. The intended and actual results of the optimization should be evaluated using an appropriate set of metrics. Use the same metrics to define the baseline and measure the achievements. Make sure that the metrics are outcome based and focused on value. Use the other guiding principles when applying this one. When optimizing and automating, it is smart to follow the other principles as well. Progress iteratively with feedback. Iterative optimization and automation will make progress visible and increase stakeholder buying for future iterations. Keep it simple and practical. It is possible for something to be simple but not optimized so use these two principles together when selecting improvements. Focus on value. Selecting what to optimize and automate and how to do so should be based on what will create the best value for the organization. Start where you are. The Technology already available in the organization may have features and functionalities that are currently untapped or underutilized. Make use of what is already there to implement opportunities for optimisation and automation quickly and economically. Let's now look at how the ITIL principles interact with and depend on each other. As well as being aware of the ITIL guiding principles, it is also important to recognize that they interact with and depend upon each other. Organisations should not use just one or two of the principles but should consider the relevance of each of them and how they apply together. For example if an organization is committed to progressing iteratively with feedback, it should also think and work holistically to ensure that each iteration of an improvement includes all the elements necessary to deliver real results. Similarly, making use of appropriate feedback is key to collaboration and focusing on what will truly be. Organizational governance is a system by which an organization is directed and controlled. Governance is realized through the following activities. The evaluation of the organization its strategy portfolios and relationships with other parties. The governing body evaluates the organization on a regular basis as stakeholders needs and external circumstances evolve. The governing body assigns responsibility for and directs the preparation and implementation of organizational strategy and policies. Strategies set the direction and prioritization for organizational activity, future investments etc. Policies establish the requirements for behavior across the organization and were relevant, suppliers, partners and other stakeholders. The governing body monitors the performance of the organization and its practices, products and services. The purpose of this is to ensure that performance is in accordance with policies and direction. The guiding principles and continual improvement to apply to all components of the SVS including governance. In an organization the governing body can adopt the ITIL guiding principles and adapt them or to find its own specific set of principles and communicate them across the organization. The governing body should also have visibility of the outcomes of continual improvement activities and the measurement of value for the organization and its stakeholders. Regardless of the scope of the SVS and the positioning of the components, it is critical to make sure that the service value chain and the organization's practices work in line with the direction given by the governing body. The governing body of the organization either directly or through delegation of authority, maintains oversight of the SVS. Both the governing body and Management at all levels maintain alignment through a clear set of shared principles and objectives. The governance and Management at all levels are continually improved to meet expectations of the stakeholders. In summary, the SVS includes the service value chain activities supported by an organization's Universal and holistic practices. The guiding principles help organizations adopt and adapt ITIL to their context. The principles include focus on value, start where you are, progress iteratively with feedback, collaborate and promote visibility, think and work holistically, keep it simple and practical, optimize and automate. Governance is realized through the activities such as evaluate, direct and monitor.

Chapter 4 The elements of ITIL 4

In the following chapters we are going to understand the ITIL 4 Framework and also understand the basic definitions of IT Service Management as defined in ITIL best practices. Before we get into understanding ITIL best practice framework let's understand the IT Service Management and its benefit by applying the best practice framework ITIL for what would be the benefits which we get. For that let us assume a scenario where two employees are discussing about advantages of adopting ITIL best practices. Why has ITIL become so popular these days? Large, medium and small organizations across the world use ITIL in order to improve the value of their services. But how can ITIL improve an organization's performance? Well, with ITIL an organization doesn't just save money but also works more effectively. It also have more benefits that are reduced IT cost, enhanced IT Services, improved productivity, better Management of business risk and service disruption, improve customer satisfaction by delivering efficient services and provides guidance to address Service Management challenges. That's great but which is the latest ITIL framework and what's new about it? Well, ITIL 4 is the latest update and ITIL has evolved from many years and ITIL 4 is the latest version and this was released in February 2019. It focuses on practical approach on how to manage the core principles of quality services, how to implement ITIL from large to small organizations and how ITIL can be utilized with frameworks such as Agile, Lean and DevOps. But what is in it for us to learn and understand from ITIL 4? Well, we are going to now look at what is ITIL 4, elements of the ITIL 4 framework that is the four dimensions and ITIL service value chain and its components, then details about ITIL 4 Certifications and companies using ITIL. But what is ITIL? ITIL is a set of framework of IT Service Management that helps in aligning IT Services with the requirements of the business, so it helps organizations to deliver IT Services using the most efficient method. ITIL's goal is to improve efficiency and achieve predictable service delivery. Finally what it means for us when we say IT Service Management or Information Technology Service Management. ITSM stands for Information Technology Service Management and it focuses on how an organization maintains IT Services for customers. Also it controls various activities involved in a process - activities like planning, designing, delivering, deploying and managing services. ITIL 4 emphasizes the importance of value creation rather than just delivering services. This involves value always as Lean - mentioned repeatedly, value should be always in customer perspective. There should be an outcome and generally we use the term called output for the products or services which are created but by using that product or services, one has to have realization of the value created by it. That request has certain outcomes. We're not speaking about just the features and function of a specific product or services, we're speaking about how the customer is benefited from that features and functionality which helps customer or consumers to realize the value. Then the creation of a value should be always with collaboration and cooperation, so ITIL 4 more emphasizes on co-creation of value. This also involves managing specific cost and risk. When we say managing specific cost and risk, it's about service provider to own the cost and risk and this cost and risk is not for the consumer or customer. Value must be clearly defined as the purpose of an organization it is to create value for its stakeholders, whereas outcome is a result of service. They are specific and help you know whether you have reached your goal. To understand the outcome of an output, let us understand an example. An output of wedding photography is the photo album but the outcome is the satisfaction that is experienced by the client when looking at the album. If the album is an output in the first case and you can see that the photos are not clear – it means poor customer experience and that would be the outcome. Similarly if the album output is very clear, the experience of the customer will be very good so that is also an outcome. Finally let's discuss the co-creation of value. In order to deliver the high quality output the service provider should maintain an interactive relationship with its stakeholders and customers, it's very essential to interact and understand the prospective view of the stakeholders and create the value accordingly. For example co-creation is a business strategy which helps consumer receives the results based on the requirements. If you take up this scenario of a restaurant where service provider provides a certain dish versus service provider provides certain facilities to the consumers of the food in the restaurant so that they will have a better experience and feedback can be provided than in there itself. This helps the restaurant personnel to work on those feedbacks and improve the service experience to the customers. The amount of money spent on specific activity or resources should be managed wisely and cost and risk of any services provided by a service provider is with the service provider. Consumer of a service just pays for a service and then as the service consumption is complete, they will just off-board themselves. Like you go and book a taxi you get on board to taxi and then you get off the taxi as you reach your destination. You will not own the vehicle, you are not owning any mobile app if you book the taxi. All the cost and risk associated with these service components would be for service provider. Another example can be that Starbucks has offered internet access to its customers which means all the associated components of the Starbucks internet services the cost and risk associated with that is owned by Starbucks. But how to identify whether a service is delivering value to customer and meeting the requirements? This can be identified by evaluating the utility and warranty. It is very essential to understand what is utility and warranty for us. Utility refers to the functionality offered by product in order to meet a specific requirement. For example utility of a training service is about the timings of the service, the content delivered during the services, the profile of the trainer etc. Whereas email services if we take as an example, utility is all those parameters features functionalities associated with the email services like mailbox capacity or the way or the speed of emails are being sent or received. Similarly warranty refers to the customer with certain assurance of the products like service availability, Information security, service capacity and service continuity. These four service availability Information security or service capacity and service continuity has to ensure the specific provided services are having those solutions which will safeguard these requirements of the services and service will become fit for use. If we take a similar example of the warranty about availability of email services, how safe is my message when I send and receive the messages - means Information security. Capacity - do I have a sufficient capacity so that all the emails can be stored. Then continuity - what happens if something goes wrong drastically. If some failure happens minimum services should be up and running so that my messaging services is on, for at least minimum need of the messaging requirements. That is about warranty. Utility refers to fit for purpose - referring to features functionality of the service whereas warranty refers to these four things availability, security, capacity and continuity making a specific services fit for use. We are going to look at

43

understanding two main elements defined in ITIL 4 that is four dimensions and ITIL service value system. The four dimensions of services involves organizations and people, Information and Technology, partners and suppliers and value streams and processes. It is always required to look at a service having a holistic picture. Having this holistic picture requires the understanding about these four dimensions of services. When I say organizations and people, Information and Technology, partners and suppliers and value streams and processes - all these four dimensions will be involved and required to look at for every services. Organizations and people refers to the organization's structure, the culture, the people, the principles and the values revolving around the people and organization structure for providing better outcomes for the services. Similarly Information and Technology involves Information and knowledge which is required along with the Technology to provide a required services and Service Management. The partners and suppliers focuses on those stakeholders who supply certain services for a service provider so that service provider can provide the better services to their consumers of the services. Value streams and processes refers to the series of steps organization takes to create deliver the products throughout the service lifecycle of services. To take an example of taxi services, who is the organization and people? The people sitting in the customer care the people like drivers the people sitting in the business people sitting in the finance people sitting in the Technology, so all these forms at an organization structure having people in it and that fulfills organization people dimension of services. Whereas Information and Technology like car itself is a Technology device Information about the schedule, or Information about the driver, similarly the Technology platform the mobile app what you use can be the one which you can visualize for Information and Technology. For partners and suppliers, generally if you look at the examples like Uber services, they are not employed by Uber. They are the partners and suppliers for providing the taxi services to Uber on behalf of Uber. Similarly internet services will be provided to by supplier so partners and suppliers involvement is essential in any services. The value streams and processes; when you open a mobile app and book a taxi you need a process which has to be established and defined and this process would trigger what vehicles are available. Similarly that process triggering to billing system, likewise many processes are connected with each other, forming a value stream to achieve a specific objective of a consumer and this involves many processes. Considering these four dimensions, every services has these four dimensions and consideration of these four dimensions are essential while strategizing services, designing services, transitioning services, delivering services and supporting the services throughout the life cycle of the services. All these four dimensions are impacted by six external factors. These six external factors can also be called as pastel factors which is political factor, economic factors, social factors, technological factors, legal factors and environmental factors. Further each dimension is affected by multiple factors. Next let's look at ITIL service value system. This forms the core part of ITIL framework. This shows an end-to-end view about what is involved in service value system. It starts with opportunity or demand and every services creating the value and continually improve to align and create the value. When I say opportunities and demand which becomes a reason for triggering an actions and activities, move from left to right. Similarly as it moves from left to right, the value is created. The term opportunity refers to the needs requirements of customers or consumers which is realized by service provider to fulfil. Whereas demand represents the requirement for products and services from the customers, so either opportunity realized by service provider which is unfulfilled need of consumers or customers, whereas demand where customer or consumer is asking and booking those products or services from you would create certain actions with the service providing organizations. Ultimately it should result in creation of those products or services with the specific features and functions. Those would enable the creation of value and also that value represents a valuable outcome. The components of service value system as we saw, guiding principles is one of that which help in providing a comprehensive vision of how an organization should manage a service. There are seven principles that is focus on value, start where you are, think and work holistically, progress iteratively with feedback, keep it simple and practical, collaborate and promote visibility and optimize and automate. When we say focus on value, which means everything we do as part of services. Every task an organization does should create value for stakeholders, especially it should increase to focus on user experience and give better consumers experience so that they can be continually the value is realized by the consumer or customers. Next principle start where you are, refers to ensuring that organization assess and analyze the scenarios to identify and improve things on a continual basis. For example organization assessing and analyzing the existing processes to identify and improve. Progress iterative and feedback; this opts for a feedback during every iterations of the work and always ensures to organize work into small and manageable sections which can lead to quick results. Collaborate and promote visibility; it is very essential to collaborate with customers, users, suppliers and all the stakeholders who are involved in services and service actions

46

as it helps in creating much better value. Think and work holistically; this creates a process that adds value to the customers or consumers and business and always helps in identification of different ways to enhance the performance of the processes because this provides the end-to-end view of services. Keep it simple and practical; it is always important to opt for minimum steps that are correct and do not add processes that create value to the stakeholders. Optimize and automate refers to the consideration of the services which needs to be optimized and automated which helps in improving the efficiency and effectiveness and also optimize the resources and costs. Next component of service value system is governance. Governance basically is responsible for evaluating, directing and monitoring the IT Service Management by adopting the guiding principles, defined in ITIL 4 framework and it may also demonstrate these principles, considering the currently available or the principles which are defined in the organization. This involves three main activities that is evaluate, direct and monitor. Evaluate refers to the performance of reviews of the services on a continual basis based on the stakeholder requirements, so how the services are performing how the new opportunities coming up would be understood and that can made visible. The directions are whatever is provided based on the evaluation done for the ITSM organization so that accordingly the required directions can be accomplished. When I say direction for example organization can have directions to enhance the business opportunities, increase the sales by 25% in coming quarter and when organization says this. In what way IT Service Management can contribute to that? In what way the readiness of IT Service Management should be when organization enhances its business to 25%? Should we optimize something with us or should we increase certain set of resources and capabilities so that increase of the business to 25% is supported or complemented by IT Service Management. As you implement that as this direction is set whether ITSM is contributing to that has to be checked monitored, so it has to monitor the performance of the organization and has to check whether the practices, the products and the services are aligned and they are in line with the direction given by the governing body. It is very essential to understand this and have this in practice so that services always continue to be aligned with the organization's business requirements and also the organizations or consumers who are using the services of a service provider. Evaluate, direct and monitor as happens regularly so that continued alignment of direction to the set direction by the governing body is ensured. The next component is service value chain which is basically a component which is which is in the middle of a service value system. This will have a set of interconnected activities that an organization performs to deliver a valuable product or services to its consumers. This will have many activities like engage, plan, improve, design and transition, obtain and build, deliver and support product and services. In the demand you don't see opportunities as it was mentioned in the service value system framework. The simple reason is that in a service value chain being part of service value system. It is always demand. When we refer to opportunities in service value system the moment it is realized there is an opportunity, the discussion happens based on that and decision happens. As the decisions happened now it is required to fulfill that demand by a service providing organization. That is the reason we don't see the word opportunity. As the demand is seen, now the engagement happens. How the engagement happens? Well, it involves planning. Planning refers to the activities, involving creating plans portfolios architectures policies which provides an organization a direction a clarity in terms of what to do. If you refer to previous version of it like ITIL v3, you can think about a service strategy part of the actions we choose to take like understanding the perspective of services, planning for the services, understanding service requirements, service level requirements which will enable to get the clarity in terms of the detail about the services and what are those results which are required to be established. People would contribute to these activities and must have great analytical and Management skills. There should be clear visualization about the services end-to-end like the principle we said having a holistic approach so unless I have a holistic picture - a bird's-eye view, I cannot understand what services is being delivered and what is that value it is going to be created. This full picture of services end-to-end has to be visualized and that is the reason plan is on the top like an umbrella so one has to understand that very clearly. As you get the insight towards that particular service, service requirement and service level requirements once the plan is ready, then you will move forward with engage - engage with the right set of stakeholders. Why should we engage with the stakeholders? Engaging with stakeholders requires clear focus on understanding the requirements as needed by the consumers. We may require to document this and we might require to understand what is that people need skills and competency in terms of engaging and we need to know and demonstrate that. So while you understand and get a good understanding about the needs of the stakeholders - stakeholders may be like end user who are using the services, customers who were discussing straight were given the requirements, whereas the suppliers who is also asking about the requirements in terms of provisioning their services to the service provider, so the engagement should go on with all those stakeholders to understand clearly and also set the expectation clearly. You may require to set an expectation to consumers, you may require to set an expectation suppliers and you are required to set an expectation to users and this has to continue throughout. So continually engaging with all the stakeholders throughout the service value system and it's very rigorous as part of service value chain. Next activity would be design and transition. Design and transition focuses on creating and releasing new and change services. When we say designing a new services we just saw like four dimensions so people, process, products and partners which is aligned to four dimensions. That is very essential to visualize and defining service solution, defining Technology architectures, defining processes, defining metrics, defining measurement methods and tools to measure that particular service and service performance is requires understanding and having those individuals who have comprehensive understanding about Service Management and they should contribute to this entire exercise of design and transitioning. Unless you have that holistic picture while planning and also well engaging to get the clarity, designing would not provide you that blueprint required. Service design package which we used as a term in ITILv3 perspective, but however the terminology would not change the blueprint the service design package what you have for a service, it is very necessary to have that in place with the detailed considerations of all the four dimensions of the services, and also considering the impact of the pastel factors. Obtain and build focuses on development and Management of the infrastructure and applications. You obtain, means you acquire resources, you acquire components - infrastructure components like servers, storage, database or application platforms, the testing platforms. You acquire, you test those and you make it ready and you set up that environment required for creation of services, transition of a services and build. Then you deliver and support. This requires to ensure that services are delivered and supported in a way that meets stakeholders expectations. As you engage on a continual basis there is a collaboration which is going on throughout and also like progress iteratively with feedback. You need to take that approach, so that you will have a feedback. By doing this you are demonstrating all the seven principles. Services provisioning is one part of it, new services provisioning or modifying the existing services to enhance the performance of the existing services with added features and functionality is one thought. Similarly, while there is an Incident, while there is a disruption, while there is a failure it is required to resolve those. Even in that scenario, one has to understand what are the impacts to the services, what are the impacts to the business and how to handle accordingly. This is true for while introducing new services and while resolving the Incidents or issues associated with the specific services which are up and running. When it is happening with the better collaboration with the customers, consumer or suppliers, every stakeholders will involve actively and they contribute as well as realize the value. It is very important that people contributing to this activity and need to be very good at prioritizing and managing complex workloads. Services such as resolving Incidents, monitoring applications and infrastructure or generating reports all these are the actions which happens as part of deliver and support. Improve every services, every service components, every processes - every individuals has to be improved. So the focus on software development and Management of cloud infrastructure and third-party services which happens as part of service value chain. This we can term it as an example where an improvement can be focused on. When I say improvement at all levels, you can think of improvement at a component level, improvement integration level, improvement at a service level or improvement at contribution to the business level, so as you go on each of these levels it is quite obvious that you need to measure the performances at each of these levels. As you measure the performances at each of these level, it provides you certain insight. Is the performance is according to what is required and what is planned, or is the services is there a deviation from the required performance. In either of these scenarios it is very essential to check and see if there is any opportunity for improvement. If things are going as planned then it's okay, so you need to identify the opportunities to improve further from that level and that would become baseline. If things are not happening the way it is planned, obviously that corrections are required. Again the improvement thought comes in. Every services at any given point in time, one has to keep seeking the opportunities for improvement and keep improving and that comes through feedback - what you get on a continual basis from the consumers and users. Next component is practices. There are around 34 Management practices which are designed to accomplish the specific objectives of services. When I say 34 practices earlier we used to have called processes which we used to say process and functions in ITIL v3 framework. ITIL v3 had defined 26 processes and five life cycle stages and also four functions. In ITIL 4 realizing that not a specific process is dedicated or associated with only one life cycle stage. Each of those processes has so much of complexity, it cannot just call as a process and it has to be called as a practice because of the complexity and transactions involved. For example if we take Incident Management, we used to call it as a process and we use to look at that as a process as part of service operation. Incident Management process as part of service operation but what are the amount of activities it involves what is the complexity of it? It goes across the various different functions so looking at this scenario where this process goes across various functions to get a result. You think of a scenario where i need to resolve Incident by doing certain changes. I trigger a Change Management and if you look at the entire framework of ITIL v3 Change Management is defined in service transition lifecycle stage. But in Operations you have Incident Management whereas Change Management is in transition, so is that service moving back to the previous lifecycle stage? That was the confusion. So instead of that if you say there is an Incident Management practice which is applicable, irrespective of the stage of that particular service, change control which is applicable across the life cycle irrespective of the scenario, the services into, so then you are not bound to any specific life cycle stage. While Incident occurs right away go and take the help of change control and then implement the required changes and then close the Incidents. This does not have any specific attachment or tying between a specific stage of the service life cycle. If you can able to recall and visualize v3 defined about five life cycle stages, first stage was service strategy having five processes, service design having eight processes, service transition having seven processes, service operation having five processes and continual service improvement having around one process aligned with CSI model continual service improvement model. Each of this process like SLA service level agreement which you which is there in service design stage so this is discussed in strategy as well and this service levels has to be monitored and managed during the service Operations and services has to be created and transitioned, aligning with the service levels defined in design. This is what the thought was, but the existence of that service level SLA service process what we used to call, was there universally across the life cycle. Initially to define next to transition next to monitor and manage so it was there. The process gets triggered some point in time but it is there throughout. In ITIL 4 this particular practice is not bound to a specific life cycle stage. whenever it is required it is triggered and each of these practices are interconnected certainly. If I take another example like Information security Management, this is also important throughout the lifecycle and very interesting part here is Information security Management practice is the one which is not just for a service provided by service provider alone. The practice of Information security should be practiced across the service provider organization so that better Information security can be provided to all the services provided by a service provider. Keeping this in mind, the 34 practices are grouped into three major categories; general Management practice, Service Management practice and technical Management practices.

Chapter 5 General Management practices

General Management practices are 14 practices that are applicable across the organization. The general Management practices are applicable across the organization and this is not bound to any specific services. For example change transformation. If you have a major change which used to call in ITIL v3 so that requires certain amount of time to move the organization thought and the culture towards certain level so that the change can become successful across the organization. Similarly to Information security Management, so many practices which are not just associated with one service can be generally applicable across the organization. 14 general Management practices are defined. Similarly that 14 general Management practices includes Information security Management, relationship Management, strategic Management, portfolio Management and as a portfolio it is a portfolio of the organization and not just about one service, architecture Management and enterprise architecture and service financial Management overall for all the services, workforce and talent Management, continual improvement, continual improvement of all the services to suit the business requirement to align and complement to the business, measurement and reporting as a whole Risk Management, knowledge Management, organizational Change Management in terms of having organizational transformation, Project Management and supplier Management. Information security Management has to focus on ensuring the safeguarding confidentiality integrity and availability of Information and Information asset of organization. Only then all that activities we do as part of this organization will be under the umbrella of Information security focus. All that we do in this organization is that we need to ensure the Information security is taken care of. People moving from entry gate to data center, so can I define that as part of for data center services? No, we have a data center facility, but someone entering the premises everyone who comes into my premises need not go to data center but they move around the data center. It's quite obvious and to safeguard someone should not tailgate without anybody's knowledge, we need to set the controls at organization level so people who are not authorized will not move towards data center. The next level of security enablement can happen exclusively for data center. That is again aligned with the framework of Information security for the organization, so it is very essential to consider this practice at the organization level, rather than just at a service level. The moment we focus at organization level, all the applicable services will also get initiated and implemented, implementation of that particular practice - that's application of that particular service as well. Similarly if you look at relationship Management - at the broader perspective relationship happens with two entities or two organizations or two individuals or two enterprises so it is of that size. It's not about one individual relationship with another individual or a service Manager has a relationship with another Manager. It is not that. It's about two entities. Service provider organization and customer organization - there should be relationship and this relationship Management also you can look at in terms of having across the organization within the various different departments and function within organization. Similarly the relationship between the Manager and subordinate or the relationship between colleagues or relation between suppliers and service providers, or relationship between service provider and customers are across. The main purpose of this is to ensure a good relationship is maintained between organizations and its stakeholders. Only then that required collaboration and transactions can happen to make the business successful. Keeping in this mind, the rest all the practices such as strategic Management or portfolio Management, architecture Management, service financial Management, workforce and talent Management, continual improvement measurement and reporting Risk Management, knowledge Management, organizational Change Management, Project Management and supplier Management are all these has to considered across. The organization perspective organization as a whole they should look at so only then the required practice of making people to understand about the dynamics of the services, dynamics of the business can be enabled. As an example if I speak about relationship Management relating to a restaurant, who has to maintain the relationship; the waiter who goes and speaks to the customer who comes to the restaurant. There should be a relationship established if not a relationship which lasts for long on one-on-one basis. It's about creation of that experience because that is one of the touch points. That is one experience what that consumer will have. The moment the consumer enters the restaurant, the people who take care of the ambience of the restaurant. If they get the right feedback in time, what kind of ambience would help? What is the feedback about the restaurant from the customer? There is a transaction and relationship which is happening similarly the people working in the kitchen versus the waiter the time they manage the Information flow from them to the waiter and then to the consumers so all a taste of the food is that customers enjoying the food - feedback going back to the kitchen and making necessary corrections there and fitting the need of the customers and consumers on a regular basis. Understanding this

57

relationship across it's obvious that the consumer of a service will have a better experience and this is not a one-time job - it should be there always and should continue throughout it is very essential to demonstrate this. Only then customer will have a better experience. Likewise all these general practices should be applicable across the organization and demonstrated so that you can create a better service experience to the consumers.

Chapter 6 Service Management practices

Service Management practices are applicable to specific services which are used for development, deployment, delivery and support in the organization's environment. When is organization it may be organization of service provider organization of consumer organization of supplier. This involves around 17 practices that is IT asset Management, monitoring and event Management, monitoring each of the service components on the service performance, business analysis, service catalog Management of all the operational services, service design, service level Management for the specific service, availability Management, capacity and performance Management, service continuity Management and Service Desk. (Remember that Service Desk was called as function when we were studying ITIL v3 but Service Desk itself is a practice where all the four dimensions is applicable, so Service Desk is also termed as practice). We also have Incident Management, Service Request Management, Problem Management, release Management, service validation and testing, service configuration Management, change control and Service Management practices. Looking at one of these practices like IT asset Management, we need to understand what is it. All those assets like server, a database, an application or an individual each of these forms services. We can also call it as configuration items. IT assets are managed throughout the life cycle of that particular IT asset and it is essential to keep those assets performance at that level so that no IT assets which are not considered are not kept without the visibility of those asset in the IT Service Management so that they are performing at certain level, ensuring the services will be performing better and that better service performance would result in better complement or contribution to the business. If we look at monitoring and event Management, now we are monitoring the services, performance of the service components and then their behaviors, the capacity to list the availability of those so we are monitoring those and learning the behavior of those service components - emphasizing on generating and detecting the status of IT Services throughout the life cycle of the service. This will keep me clear, providing that better picture so that we will have a clarity in terms of what needs to be addressed at what point in time. Today's monitoring and event Management tools are so capable compared with the way it was there like 15-20 years back, bringing automation to it and already lot of tools are automated that way which provides predictive analysis which would provide the required action to improve the experience of the services. Focusing on this monitoring and event Management need of a specific service. What needs to be looked at something which is non-acceptable behaviour. What is that we can term it as something which is okay this is how the behavior should be. That needs to be understood correctly and then whenever the deviation occurs, monitoring and event Management would throw an alert, at the same time it will also keep analyzing the trend of it and providing necessary insight towards what actions needs to be taken. Likewise each of these practices specific to each of the services has to be looked at carefully and demonstrated. While doing this one should not ignore the fact that alignment to those seven principles defined.

Chapter 7 Technical Management practices

Technical Management practices refers to the Management of Technology domains for the Service Management purposes by expanding or shifting their focus from Technology solutions to IT Services. If I am just looking at a server for example an application for example as an individual component, so I am not seeing entire service as a whole, but my focus being on that individual IT component is also essential - I cannot ignore that part. The technical Management practices have three types which includes deployment Management, software development and Management infrastructure and platform Management. Overall general Management practices 14, Service Management practices 17 and technical Management practices 3 hence totally 34 Management practices defined in ITIL 4. As you design and transition obtain and build to deliver you need to deploy. While deploying that deployment has to be scheduled like release scheduling we do. Once that is scheduled then deployment would happen at certain point in time, so deployment practice would help in terms of designing and managing and controlling the build test and deployment of releases in order to deliver new functionality required by the business. This is for a specific service or something which needs to be transitioned or implemented as part of the service life cycle where you need a specific technical or technological actions and those needs to be complied with. Similarly if you speak about software development and Management it would focus on enhancing the quality of software development and ensures to provide the required functionality for IT Services. Specific practice depending on the kind of platforms which are used, similarly for infrastructure and platform Management. A question may arise here we are speaking about the practices which are general, which are service specific which are technically but what about the people? People are also a resource. As the overall practices what we have - all these are done by people, so one has to look at having enhancing the capabilities of the individuals which are required to demonstrate all of these activities. That is definitely one important focus which specifically it may not mention but it is very essential to have those individuals. Various roles where it can comes across like service Manager, process owner or service owner which we used to see as a designation and also roles of Service Management. Those roles needs to have a specific required competencies and capabilities, only then they can perform as part of these practices.

Chapter 8 Change Management

Change Management handles change to service asset and configuration item or CI baselines across the whole service lifecycle. The purpose of the Change Management process is to control the life cycle of all changes and help in implementing beneficial changes with minimum disruption to IT Services. The objective of Change Management is to respond to business and IT requests to ensure alignment of services with business needs, ensure that changes are introduced in a controlled manner, optimizing business risk, ensure timely and successful implementation of changes to meet business needs and use standard processes and record every change. The scope of Change Management is to handle changes to architecture, tools, metrics, processes and documentation, addition, removal or modification of a service or a CI or associated documentation and changes to any of the five aspects of service design. The Change Management process starts with the request for change or RFC. The RFC is logged in the Change Management system and the Information is captured and tracked to completion. An initial review is performed to filter RFC's that are incomplete or incorrectly routed. The RFCs are then assessed which may require the involvement of the change advisory board or the emergency change advisory board for business justification, impact, cost, benefit and risk associated with the changes. Next, the change is authorized by the change Manager. The change requester in turn will ensure that they have the approval in the following three areas. Financial; what is it going to cost and what is the cost of not doing it. Business; what are the consequences is to the business both of implementing and not implementing the change and Technology; what are the consequences to IT infrastructure.

Following this Change Management coordinates the work performed with multiple checkpoints and forwards approved changes to the relevant product experts to build and test the changes and create and deploy releases. Finally, the implemented changes are reviewed in a post implementation review or PIR. If the change is successful it can be closed. A key activity of Change Management is the assessment of the change request either by the change Manager or the change advisory board. The seven R's of Change Management a set of seven questions forming a quick checklist to assess the impact and risk to benefit ratio of a change are who raised the change, what is the reason for the change, what is the required return, what are the risks involved, what resources are required to deliver the change, who is responsible for building, testing and implementing the change, what is the relationship between this change and other changes. A metric or a Key Performance Indicator or KPI is used to measure and report performance to manage a process, IT Service or activity. KPIs are selected in a way that ensures efficiency and cost effectiveness. Some of the metrics used in Change Management are for compliance, decrease in the number of unauthorized changes, decrease in the number of emergency changes, whether the integrity of the CIS is maintained, for effectiveness and delivering value increase in the percentage of changes implemented that meet customer requirements, reduction in disruptions defects and rework, reduction in failed or backed out changes, decrease in the quantity of Incidents attributable to any change, for efficiency, benefits gain that is the value of the change compared to the cost incurred to implement the change, average time to implement the change by urgency, priority or type, increase in the percentage accuracy of change estimates. The key challenges faced by Change Management are the following.

- Business pressure; there's pressure to immediately implement any new business process initiatives in the organization.
- Incomplete and inaccurate configuration Management system leading to inaccurate change assessment.
- Technical function areas working in silos.
- Lack of communication channels between the technical teams and other teams involved in service delivery make it difficult to execute a change.
- Misunderstanding of emergency changes. Sometimes the technical team may misunderstand between urgency of implementing a change and emergency changes.
- Scalability in a large organization is a challenge as some CIS may not be deployable in the existing infrastructure - making it difficult for the Change Management team to implement the change.
- Vendor or contract compliance. In case vendors have a Change Management system of their own, they may resist from the Change Management process in the business organization.

Chapter 9 Incident Management

The process of handling all Incidents throughout their lifecycle from when they are first reported to when they are either resolved or nothing more can be done in relation to them is known as Incident Management. Incidents are raised over the phone, over emails and through web-based and event Management tools. The purpose of Incident Management is to help restore service Operations to normal as soon as possible to minimize adverse impacts on business Operations and ensure the best possible service quality and availability. The primary objective of Incident Management is to standardize methods and procedures used for the efficient and prompt response of IT Services. Incident Management increases the visibility of Incident communication to business and IT support staff. In addition, it aligns Incident Management activities and priorities with those of the business. The scope of Incident Management is to manage any disruption or potential disruption to live IT Services. It also includes events identified directly by users through the Service Desk, identified through an interface between the event Management and Incident Management tools and those reported or logged by technical staff. Incident Management adds a lot of value to business. It lowers business downtime which in turn leads to higher availability of the services. It allows the business to better identify priorities and dynamically allocate resources as required. Let us look at an example illustrating the importance of Incident Management. Let us understand this with a scenario. Imagine an IT Service provider without an Incident Management plan in place - only IT support staff. In the absence of Incident Management issues are handled on a first-come first-served basis. This means if there are 10 issues related to printing the IT support staff are occupied with resolve those issues. At this time, the major business service becomes unavailable, there's no IT support available to respond. On the other hand, if the IT Service provider uses Incident Management, printer calls will be prioritized slow and fewer resources will be allocated to resolving them. This ensures that if a high-priority Incident occurs, focus can be shifted immediately to resolve the high-priority Incidents and manage printer users with minimum resources. Another way Incident Management adds value to a business is by increasing the ability to identify potential improvements to services. Now let's discuss the basic concepts of Incident Management. Some of the basic concepts of Incident Management are timescales, Incident models and major Incidents. The objective of Incident Management is to restore services as soon as possible. It is important to decide the timescales for Incident resolution. The business defines the time skills while setting up a service. To commit to such timescales the service provider and the customer must agree and document it in the service level agreements. Timescales depend on the defined Incident priority and are documented in the operational level agreements and underpinning contracts or UCs. Service Management tools are used to automate timescales and to escalate the Incident as required, based on a set of predefined rules. When an Incident occurs for the first time and has a major impact, a procedure is set up so that any future recurrence can be handled effectively. This procedure is now called an Incident model. A major Incident is a break in service which threatens to cause or is causing loss to the business. If not given immediate attention, the major Incident may even lead to huge loss. The loss could be financial or in terms of brand image. A separate procedure with shorter time scales and a greater urgency is used for major Incidents. Next let's discuss the Incident Management process flow. The Incident Management process flow is described as follows. Identification; here the Incident is detected or reported through event Management. Alternatively, the impacted user registers it through a web interface over a phone call or through email. Registration; here the Incident is logged and the record is created. Incident categorization; the registered Incident is categorized according to type, status, impact, urgency or SLA. If the issue reported is not an Incident but a request from the user or a change proposal, it is handled according to the request fulfillment process. Prioritization; once the Incident has been categorized, it is assigned a prioritization code which indicates the handling procedure to use. Internet priority is decided based on the impact and urgency of the issue. Functional escalation; after prioritization an initial diagnosis is carried out to discover all the symptoms of the Incident. If the Service Desk cannot resolve the Incident, it's escalated for further support in a process called a functional or horizontal escalation. Functional escalation is based on knowledge or expertise. Hierarchical escalation; if the nature of the Incidents is more serious, the appropriate IT Managers are notified. This is called as hierarchical or vertical escalation. Vertical escalation is used when the existing resolution of an Incident is not satisfactory to the end user. Investigation; if no escalation is required and there is no known solution, the Incident is investigated for a new solution. This type of investigation can also occur in a functional escalation. Resolved; on finding the solution it is applied to resolve the issue. Closed; if the Incident is fully resolved, the service recovers to a fully functional level and the Incident is closed.

Chapter 10 Problem Management

The process of managing problems and coming up with workarounds for them is called Problem Management. In the context of ITIL, a problem is the cause of one or more Incidents or potential Incidents. The cause may not be known at the time of Incidents occurrence. Problems are initially classified as Incidents and are documented in problem records. A workaround is a temporary way to restore service failures to an operational level. Example is rebooting a server. The reason behind the servers failure may not be known however on rebooting the service can be restored. Workarounds are used for reducing or eliminating the impact of an Incident or problem for which a full resolution is not yet available. Workarounds for problems are documented in known error records and workarounds for Incidents that do not have associated problem records are documented in the corresponding Incident records. Incident or problem records are created in the Service Management tool. Once a problem is identified based on its priority, effort is directed towards finding the root cause. A temporary fix or a workaround might be used to restore services to a usable level for the time being. The moment a workaround or an unresolved root cause to the problem is found, it becomes a known error and IT Services are aware of the issue. Known errors are managed throughout their lifecycle with the Problem Management process. Development teams or suppliers may also identify known errors. For example application and compatibility reports for Windows by Microsoft. A database is created for known errors workarounds and their solutions. This database is called known error database or KEDB. It helps in faster diagnosis and resolution of Incidents. Priority means the relative importance of an Incident, problem or change. It is used to identify required times for action to be taken. For example the service level agreement or SLA may state that priority two Incidents must be resolved within 12 hours. Priority is calculated based on the impact and urgency of the issue. Impact is the measure of the effect the issue has on the business processes of IT Service support. Urgency is how soon the issue can be handled. Priority equals impact, plus urgency.

Chapter 11 ITIL 4 Foundation Guiding Principles

Our next topic is going to be the guiding principles and it's going to be worth 6 questions on the actual exam so it's a bit more important to know about these. The guiding principles are recommendation according to ITIL that can guide a specific organization or any organization under any circumstances. It doesn't matter what you are trying to achieve and it doesn't matter what projects you are running or how your organization is built up, these guiding principles generally apply to any industry, any service provider and any organization and even for the implementation of ITIL for itself. First one is focus on value. Everything we are doing within the organization should be somehow focused on value. It should somehow create directly or indirectly value for any stakeholder. If we are doing something which is not generating any value for anybody, we should question why are we still doing that because it might be a very old thing that we have always been doing things like this. Probably heard sentences like that and that's the kind of stuff we should get rid of if we don't need it anymore. So anything you are doing it should somehow be valuable to somebody. The next one is start where you are which is all about thinking about our current situation before we jump into anything big. When we are running a project we might want to have a look at what we already have in place like in a resources, server capacity, people's knowledge and stuff like that. Try to reuse our existing resources whenever possible instead of reinventing the wheel all the time over and over again. I have seen this in real life far too often so I would strongly advise to have a quick look and do some baseline assessment and understand your current situation before you are trying to evolve and go into a new situation and improve into a new situation. We can talk about progress iteratively with feedback. If you are familiar with Agile this is probably going to ring some bells because it is all about this iterative approach of continuously building and delivering stuff. Not planning the big deal like in waterfall Project Management, rather do small steps and have a continuous learning experience and get a lot of lot of feedback from your customers and stakeholders. This one says don't do everything at once, take the baby steps instead and try to get as much feedback as possible from your customers and stakeholders because those are most valuable learning points for you. Collaborate and promote visibility is all about collaboration as it already says. It's all about cooperation and co-creation of value. It's all about involving the right people on customer side on our side as a service provider and also on stakeholder side or supplier side to get the right and factual data which helps us to take the right decisions in the end. Let's say I'm a Manager. How am I supposed to take any kind of decision if I don't have factual and correct data on my table? We need to measure and we need to get the help of different stakeholders and parties in a service provider and other organizations and then once we have that data, I can take informed decisions based on that data. A very strong tool now that is available for promotion of visibility is a common board. You might be working in Agile environments so you already know about that because frameworks Scrum more Safe are also using it but it's a big visual Information radiator or beaver and it's all about making sure that we can visualize all the things that our team or organization is working on and is displayed on this board. You can do it digitally but most of the people are doing it on an actual physical board with sticky notes and it helps to visualize what is happening within that team, and that helps also further the completion of the job. Think and work holistically is all about having an understanding of the big picture because nothing in the service provider or customer organization ever stands alone. There is no single component which is not somehow connected to other components. The best to think about this would be a CMDB or Configuration Management Database. Nothing is ever standing alone so if we want to run a successful initiative like a project or an improvement, we need to have an understanding about how the components which we try to improve or upgrade are connected to other components. I'm not just talking about technical stuff here. I'm also talking about people or knowledge, technical stuff like configuration items, software, servers or whatever it is. So we need to understand the bigger picture of how our initiative or our work is going to make the whole better. Don't promote silo thinking because that happens far too often that Managers only think about their own little department or their own little team and how to make themselves look good, instead of considering the good of the whole company. In the end we are sitting in the same boat so we want to pull the same strings and row in the same direction and that only happens if I have an understanding of the big picture, even though I don't need to have all the details about every other part of the machinery or every other gear. It's enough to have a holistic understanding on a high level.

Keep it simple and practical speaks for itself. It just says that we shouldn't over complicate stuff. If something can be done the easy way, why should we choose the hard way. Nevertheless, I've seen this happening a lot of times that people over complicate things just because their technical expertise makes it possible and they want to look good because they can accomplish this super complex thing. But in the end it doesn't make any sense. It's a waste of resources so use the least possible steps to achieve your goal whatever you are doing and think about the outcomes because if you focus on outcomes, it will help you understand the necessary steps to get that outcome or output. Don't think about all the steps upfront. Think about what is it I need to achieve and think about what is the easiest way to achieve this. Bill Gates once said that he will always hire a lazy person to do a difficult job at Microsoft. Why? Well because he says that a lazy person will find an easy way to do it. In the end it's kind of true although it sounds a little bit drastical now, but the essence of it is still applicable. Try to use the least possible steps to accomplish your goal instead of over complicating things. Last but not least let's talk about optimize and automate, which is all about maximizing the value of human work by automating everything else as far as possible. Sometimes it doesn't make sense to automate everything because it can be very costly, but it makes sense to do the robot work which is repeatable which happens a lot all the time - that can be automated. You can use software applications like automated testing tools which help you reduce the need of human interference and they are also much faster than involving human which allows the people then to concentrate or much more important work. For example they could be developing things or doing other things which are more valuable to the organization.

Chapter 12 ITIL 4 Foundation Continual Improvement as a Practice

These practices are important so please really pay attention here. The first one is continual improvement as a practice. First of all you need to know that continual improvement happens everywhere in the organization or I would say should happen at every level of the organization. That's why we have it in a service value system. There is a continual improvement part of it. We have it in a service value chain because there is an activity called improve and we also have it as a practice continual improvement and that's what we're going to talk about now. You also need to know that there will be a lot of improvement ideas in a company. You have probably a lot of people in your organization and all of them might be coming up with new ideas, so it's important to know that these ideas need to be reprioritized when new ones are added into the continual improvement register, but you could also call it an idea backlog which could be a Kanban board or it could be an idea box. Continual improvement is the responsibility of everyone. Organizations may have a continual improvement team for better coordination, especially bigger organizations might have something like an innovation team. I've been working for a company which had a team which was continuously searching the market for new technologies and new startup companies, having good ideas to see if anything can be integrated into our own organization which totally makes sense to be still be competitive and keep being competitive on the market. Also important all four dimensions need to be considered during any improvement initiative. Value streams and processes, Information and Technology, organization and people and partners and suppliers; these are the four most basic building stones for any organization so if we are running an improvement initiative, we are building on those four building blocks. Continual improvement is a practice as well and if you have been doing ITIL version three, this might seem familiar to you because it's a continual improvement model, although it has been slightly updated since version 3 of ITIL. It starts with what is the vision, like the business vision or our mission of the company, the goals and objectives that we want to achieve because we need to have an understanding of the high-level goals of the company before we are running any initiative for improvement, so we can align the vision and mission of our improvement with the vision and mission of the whole organization. We want to make sure that we are doing the right thing and we are not just wildly improving something that nobody wants in the end. The next question is; where are we now? We need to perform baseline assessments and we need to measure to understand our current situation, and we even have a guiding principle for this one. It's called start where you are which helps us understand our current situation and helps us understand if we have the possibility to reuse anything. In this continual improvement model, the where are we now question is about the starting point of our improvement journey. If you are doing a trip on Google Maps it would be your where am I now or current location. Next question is where do we want to be? There will be our destination in Google Maps. We need to define measurable targets and I'd like to stress the fact that they need to be measurable, shorter-term targets. Because what is the vision is more about long-term targets and where do we want to be in the next couple of years. But where do we want to be is about shorter term targets like milestones that we need to achieve which are getting us to the overall long-term goals. So where do we want to be is all about measurable targets and they need to be SMART. Probably you have already heard that term. If not, SMART stands for specific, measurable, achievable, relevant and time box or time bound. Question number four is how do we get there? We need to have a defined improvement plan in place. We need to think about how do we want to achieve our measurable targets. How do we want to get there? It means we need to have an idea of we want to do it if we want to do it Agile or Waterfall, how we want to set up our teams, how we set up our Management structures. The next step would be and that's the change to version 3 of ITIL is take action. It's all about making sure that we act on our plan for improvement. We really do, instead of just doing the planning and doing the thinking and so on we really take action so we execute the improvement plan. Then we need to keep asking ourselves did we get there? Let's say we have defined a measurable target in the where do we want to be step, which says that by the end of the year, we want to increase income by 10%. Kind of measurable - it's a SMART goal. We say did we get there? The year-end has arrived so now we need to evaluate our metrics and KPIs and we have set up before our measurable targets and we need to see if we were able to achieve the goal. If yes, cool. If no, why? There needs to be kind of a lesson learned. The last question is how do we keep the momentum going? How can we keep that cool improvement up? How do we make sure that we are not going back to the old practices of working? How do we make sure that we can continue our improvement journey to keep the speed up and to make sure that if we improved something, people not just go back to how it was before, because there is a tendency for that and there is a topic which is called organizational Change Management helping with this a lot.

Chapter 13 ITIL 4 Foundation Information Security Relationship and Supplier Management

On the actual exam you're going to have five questions on other practices so let's jump right into it. First of all, we're going to have Information security Management. It is an important practice because it makes sure that data and Information which we are handling throughout our daily operation is protected against any kind of hazard like leaking or hacking, so it protects Information needed by organizations to conduct business. Let's face it. In the end it's one of our most important commodities. Any company working with IT or providing IT Services is centered around Information. In some form or in some way we are handling customer data and Information so we need to ensure the confidentiality, integrity, availability, authentication or authenticity and non-repudiation of the data we are handling. Confidentiality means that only people who are approved to have access, have access. Integrity means that the data cannot just be changed by running people. It is complete and it is accurate. Availability means well it's available when it's needed by whom it's needed. Authentication means that we can uniquely identify people in our systems which means that we have user accounts with unique IDs and non-repudiation means that Information cannot just be changed without a trace. That transactions cannot just simply be reverted without having or leaving a mark somewhere in the system. The next one is relationship Management. The goal here is to establish and nurture links between organizations and different organizational units and their stakeholders as strategic and tactical and also operational level. It's not written but it still falls under that scope as well. We try to make sure that we find the best possible ways to communicate and collaborate with our internal and external stakeholders because we're going to have a lot of them, so we might want to focus on how to effectively and efficiently work together with them. Relationships are identified, they are analysed, monitored and wherever possible improved. That's a kind of life cycle in relationship Management and you want to remember this one for the exam. Then we have supplier Management. That one ensures that suppliers of the organization third parties, externals and their performances are managed to support a seamless service provision to our own customers. We're going to have tons of suppliers and companies who provide something to us and we need to make sure that whatever they are providing is according to the agreements which we have with them, which we call underpinning contracts. Before in the end the goal of this practice is that we get what we paid for from our vendors and suppliers

Chapter 14 ITIL 4 Foundation IT Asset Monitoring & Event and Release Management

IT asset Management plans and manages the full lifecycle of our IT assets with the goal to maximizing their value control their cost because there will be some which are quite costly and to support decision-making about should we reuse our assets or maybe we need new assets. Depends on the situation but there is the guiding principle start where you are which says that we should try to reuse whenever whatever possible. By definition and you should remember this, an IT asset is any financially valuable component. It can contribute to the delivery of IT products or services, and I like to highlight the fact that we are talking about financially valuable components. The focus is on the finances. Monitoring and event Management is all about recognizing events happenings in the IT infrastructure and making sense of them to decide what we should do with them. It observed services and components and records changes in their state. It identifies those events, categorizes them and establishes standard responses. These standard responses could be Incident or Service Requests or changes or whatever alerts in a system but they need to be categorized and established. By definition it's important an event is any change of state that has a significance for the Management of a configuration item of service, so anything that could be happening and you can imagine in the life of the service provider organization there are quite a lot. So an event could be that somebody logs into a server. An event could be that somebody has changed a password or log the ticket or use their badge on the door. There are a lot of different things but an event could also be let's say that there is an alert that the hard drive of a server is almost full or that the CPU utilization is over 90%. So we need to categorize them and according to ITIL and you might also be familiar from previous versions we have three types of Informational event where we don't really need to do anything - kind of goes into a lock file it can be read if needed but it doesn't really have any huge significance. Then we have warnings. Those are these events where thresholds are breached like what I mentioned before hard drive almost full or CPU utilization very high. These cases we should do something because if we don't do anything, it will come to exceptions. Exceptions are the types of events which have happened but should not have happened - mainly issues and we certainly need human intervention to straighten them out again and usually these are handled in the form of the Incident Management practice. Let's have a quick look at release Management which makes sure that new or change services and features are available for use. Releases have been decoupled from deployments but first let's have a quick look at the definition of a release which is a version of a service or another configuration item or a collection of configuration items that is made available for use. It's really made available for use so people see it have it available and can start working with that. In ITIL 3 we had release an employment Management and it was kind of the same process but here we have two separate practices and release Management has been decoupled from deployment Management to allow us the cannery or dark releases. That's a kind of stuff where we move something into production but we don't show it to people because we have a switch on it or a feature toggle and that allows us to push something into production but still run some tests on it with a limited user base before we make it available to the whole user base in the end.

Chapter 15 ITIL 4 Foundation Service Configuration and Deployment Management

Service configuration Management ensures accurate Information is available when needed about services, configuration items and their relationships. That's quite important. Previously it has been called service a certain configuration Management in ITIL version 3 but as you can see it has also been separated. Before we have talked about asset Management and now we have conflict Management. Config Management is all about making sure we have an understanding of the overall picture of our infrastructure and that we understand what components we have in there and how they relate and connect to each other. These components they're called configuration items or CIs. A configuration item is any component that needs to be managed to deliver an IT Service - whatever it is, could be technical component but it could also be logical component. Some companies even keep track of the skills employees have within their organization because those are also configuration items. For example somebody has knowledge about ITIL 4 or somebody knows about DevOps or somebody knows how to program in Java and so on. We also have CMDBs and these are Configuration Management Databases which are actual databases or collections of databases, holding all the configuration items and their connections. These are physical databases and not really useful to look at or not really nice to look at and that's why we also need so-called CMS's, configuration Management systems which are technically front-ends or user interfaces for the CMDBs like all the ticketing solutions you can find out there for ticket handling. You have the possibility to attach assets to the ticket and that is because they are acting as a configuration

Management system, while they are at data in the underlying Configuration Management Databases. Deployment Management is all about moving new or changed hardware software documentation or any other component from one environment to the next. So let's say in your application environment you have a Dev environment a test environment like a QA and a prod environment, so anytime you have developed something on Dev you need to move it to QA for testing then it's going to be deployment Management and then once it's tested and everything is fine you're going to move it to prod now if you make it available in prod for usage or not that's a question of release Management. But the pure movement of code and configuration is a responsibility of deployment Management. DevOps plays a huge role here with the help of DevOps we can reach continuous delivery and continuous integration where the developer builds the change in Dev which is automatically tested and moved to the next environment until it arrives in prod. It can be amazing. You look at huge companies like Amazon. Just a little example here which is fun, Amazon reached a technical level where they have one of the highest release rates in history. It's every 2.4 seconds, they release some stuff into production. It's amazing. I understand it's a huge platform but still in every 2.4 seconds they have something new in production – Wow! Kudos Amazon! But what I want to say is that deployment does not equal release any more since we have the possibility with Cannery releases to separate those.

Chapter 16 ITIL VS IT Service Management

Perhaps you've seen or heard about ITIL or someone has recommended that you look into this very amazing framework that rules in the world of IT Service Management. Well, glad you're along for the ride and let's start off with the basics. Essentially ITIL is a set of best practices and guidance in IT Service Management. It helps define the direction of the service provider with a clear capability model and it aligns them to business strategy into customer needs, plus it helps us speak a common language of IT Service Management with a universal glossary of terms. ITIL has led the IT Service Management industry with guidance, training and Certification programs for over 30 years. But what in the world is an ITIL? Well ITIL is an acronym it stands for Information Technology Infrastructure Library. Yup, that's right – library. In today's cloud-based digital world that can be a bit of an archaic reference but back in the 1980s the British Government noticed something about IT. Millions of pounds were being spent on Technology and they weren't really sure that their citizens, government, offices and officials were receiving any value from these purchases and uses and what they understood even back then was that it's not about the Technology - it's how you use the Technology that provides the outcomes that the customers or consumers are looking for, so they produced books. Thus a library that explain how to create processes things like how to handle an Incident, how to perform Change Management, how do you maintain a service catalog that lists all the services you offer, and at one point there were about 30 booklets or so that dealt with many of the processes and practices an it organization would use to align the IT department with the business. Around 2000 so fast forward a little bit from the 80s the over 30 booklets were consolidated down to eight books but there were two books; Service Support and Service Delivery that were the primary focus. Then in 2007 version 3 was published that took the eight books into five equally weighted books based on things like service strategy, service design, transition, Operations and all these things. In 2011 a major update was published. This update stuck with the same fundamental concepts that were released under version 3 but 2011 cleared up a lot of inconsistencies and ambiguities that came out in 2007 and they also dropped the whole versioning thing. It's no longer version two or version three - it was just ITIL 2011. In 2018 ITIL 4 was announced and in early 2019 ITIL 4 Foundation was released - bringing us up to where we are today. Notice I called it a framework. ITIL embraces a practical approach to Service Management. It says do what works and what works is adapting a common framework of practices that unite all areas of IT Service provision towards a single aim that of delivering value to the business. There are a few things that do make it successful. Number one, ITIL has a focus on customer experience. They also make sure that we build value streams and move our organizations towards a digital transformation and even embracing new ways and methodologies - things like Lean, Agile, DevOps, plus ITIL is vendor neutral. It doesn't matter if you have products such as Cisco or Juniper, Microsoft or Ubuntu, AWS or Google Cloud, ITIL works in all infrastructure environments. It's also non-prescriptive. It uses globally accepted best practices. If you don't want to follow ITIL's suggested process or practice as they presented, that's fine - do what works. However you are encouraged to embrace how ITIL recommends building out your IT environment as these are best practices from all parts of the world and all kinds of different industries and that can help your organization be the best at what you do. ITIL represents the learning experiences and thought leadership of the world's best in-class service providers.

Chapter 17 Change Management Process in 5 Steps

There was one word that I used to dread and no it wasn't endoplasmic reticulum - the word was change. Change meant risk, risk meant threats to the success of my project or at a minimum missing my deadlines, shooting past my budget numbers. But in reality, change is going to happen. You can grate your teeth and bear it or you can embrace it and use it to make your IT Services or projects that much better. As we look at today's IT projects in IT Services, we see a much more Agile approach to things and in this chapter we're not going to dive into change in the world of Agile with Spikes or Scrum, instead we're going to look at the Change Management process in a more traditional mode. This doesn't mean that it isn't useful in your environment. In fact the principle and theory behind Change Management or Change Enablement as ITIL 4 calls it is sound even in the Agile world so let's break this down. Change means risk so one of the first things you'll really want to have in place to have a successful Change Management process in Project Management and IT Service Management Risk Management. That is a whole another topic but if you don't have Risk Management of some kind, look to see if you can't get that in place quickly. When it comes to all the different standards and frameworks, you're going to notice that all of them follow a pretty simple pattern. All change should start with a RFC or request for change. In that RFC should be several pieces of Information that will be added to your change log documentation. Things like the who is asking for the change. That's really important. Is it the customer? Is it the CEO or perhaps it's the network Operations guy? But no matter what, all RFCs should be documented and all stakeholders should be able to submit a change request so we need to know what areas are affected as well so we need to put down. Is it hardware? Is it software? Is it workforce? Some people will also want to categorize their changes like standard changes versus emergency changes. Setting good criteria and clarifying how and when they should be submitted can be a big help here. It's at this step that we also prioritize our RFCs if we have a whole bunch of them. In ITIL 4 we break them up by impact and urgency and then next, what we're going to do is have some impact analysis and here's where you see Professional Change Management people shine. It's not rocket science. Unless you work for Elon Musk in SpaceX, then it might be about rocket science. But if you understand the competing constraints of cost, time, quality, risk and scope it's not that difficult so let's take an RFC. Let's say that you are working on an infrastructure project where they're installing a new system. The original specs said that the hardware needs to be hardwired to the network, however you find out that there might be some historical buildings that you are putting some of this equipment into and using wireless might be less expensive and a better option so we have a change. We need to do that impact analysis based on the competing constraints. Will it be more or less expensive to go wireless? Will it shorten the schedule since we don't have to run cabling in those buildings or maybe make it longer? What will the quality be like now that we aren't hardwired? Is it more secure to do wireless or less? By using the constraints we can do the risk analysis as well as understand the complete impact of implementing the change. Once you've analyzed the situation, you need to decide; is it approved or is it denied. If it's denied, it's really important to document the whys of the denial. This is going to help in the long term projects or delivery of IT Services as there might be someone later on that thinks of the same idea for change. By having all of that Information at your fingertips in the documentation, you can decide whether to maybe analyze it again. Maybe some time has gone by might be wanting to look at that a little bit or simply point to the original denied decision. But let's say that wireless change looks good from a budget, schedule and quality focus. You will approve the change and then hand it off to the appropriate team to implement the change. Implementation can be a simple flick of a switch or it might require more in-depth planning. Regardless, this is where the rubber meets the road of that decision that you've made and can also introduce some more risks that weren't identified before, so keep your eyes open and listen to those people that are doing the implementation. There might need to be some slight modifications to that original RFC. If they go out of tolerance, you might need to stop that change resubmit the RFC for further analysis based on the data that you've picked up in that initial implementation. Finally there is the review and reporting stage. This is where you look back and you see how successful that change was as well as maybe doing a retrospective or lessons learned. Never just implement the change and then just keep on going. The more you learn from successful and failed implementations, the smoother and less disruptive the future changes will be. Then it's time to start all over with more changes. I understand how disruptive change can be to your operational routines and just day-to-day keeping things running, but the beauty of Technology and why most of us chose this industry is that there is always something new, plus if you can get a good Change Management or Enablement process in place, it won't be as disruptive as it was before. Your projects will be more successful, your IT Services will be delivered with value and that's awesome.

Chapter 18 Project Management vs. Service Management

Are you confused about the differences between Project Management and Service Management? Well, in this chapter I'm going to explain the different career paths, Certifications and processes that set these two amazing fields apart. Quite frankly what's the big deal? Both are near and dear to my heart. But quite frankly they're not that much different and they can complement one another. But they are different in their focus and approach. Before comparing the two we should first understand what exactly the two terms mean. Start off with Project Management. It primarily focuses only on the project and on what's really happening right there. It's all about the application of techniques and knowledge for following laid down plans and that can be big plans like in a waterfall or a small plans or sprints for Agile and we follow those plans and meet the expectations of customers and stakeholders alike. On the other hand, we have Service Management. This is a process based practice that focuses on delivering IT Services that benefit customers. It aligns the delivery of the IT Services with the needs of an organization that uses them. For our intents and purposes we focus on the IT side of things and you might hear it called IT Service Management or ITSM. But what are the other differences when we talk about these two things?

	Project Management	Service Management
Focus	Individual projects	Management & Delivery of IT services
Duration	Temporary process until project is complete	Permanent process
Potential Issues	Suppliers, risks, communication channels, procurement, team building , timing, etc.	Inadequate staff, poor planning and designing, lack of communication among others, etc.
Process	Initiation, planning, execution, monitoring, and closing a particular project	Designating, creating, delivering, supporting and managing overall lifecycle of services
Benefits	Improving chances of achieving desired goal, set scope, growth and development within team	Provides value, improve efficiency, reduce operational cost, improve effectiveness, improve visibility, etc.
Objective	Complete temporary projects simply to deliver and achieve desired goal	Ensure a correct process, technology and team members are put in place
Certifications	PMP, PRINCE2®, etc	ITIL®, COBIT, SIAM, etc.
Types	Agile & Waterfall	Lifecycle & Value System Approach
Uses	Uses five processes	Uses 34 Practices, Value Streams, Governance

You look at this and will see that we've got everything from Project Management which focuses primarily on individual projects. Then you have IT Service Management or Service Management that focuses on the Management and Delivery of the services that you might have created as a project. The duration is another big one. For Project Management they are temporary endeavors to produce a unique product, service or result. There's a beginning and there's an end. Where a Service Management has more of an ongoing operational type of thing that once you start delivering the services you want to continue to deliver the services. The processes and there's five of them and we'll talk a little bit about that later on. As well as in Service Management where you have all these different practices that you would follow to help make sure that the operation, the delivery and the value of those services does take place. There are benefits by looking at something as a project because it does have a beginning and an end. You can focus on that. Depending on whether you use a predictive waterfall approach to Project Management where you do a lot of planning up front and then change takes a little bit more to get accomplished. Or whether you use more of an Agile approach which is going to be very small what they call sprints where you take small bits of work, work on it review it see how well it worked if you need to redo it. You can. If not, you move on pull some Information from the backlog and off you go and finish that particular project. Very good for software development. Where you have the benefits of IT Service Management is where you give that value co-creation. Where the service provider and the service consumer work together to not only deliver but also receive the services and make sure that everybody's getting what they need. It could be anything from profits for the service provider to needs where I need outcomes that I'm trying to achieve as a service consumer. We also have the objectives and that are slightly different and the Certifications. Why don't we go ahead and give you an example of maybe how this might work in an organization. Let's take Elon Musk's very cool company called Tesla. When Elon and let's face it his Design and Development team created the new Cybertruck or we would say any of the other new models that initial creation was a project. It had a beginning and it had an end and it definitely created what many people would call a unique product service or result. But once that project was finished and you have your new shiny Cybertruck, Service Management or in the case of something like a Cybertruck, IT Service Management steps in. There are constant feature of updates, software patches. Maybe there's some bugs in the system that need to be fixed. There's customer support; I need to have it repaired or where can I find the latest you know plug in stations and get my car my Cybertruck charged up. And don't forget that Tesla as a company has internal systems and services that allow them to support the different models of vehicles and even those solar power cell systems that they install on houses. They're closely related but there are real differences in the two different modalities.

Something else that shows the differences are what we would call the KPIs or Key Performance Indicators.

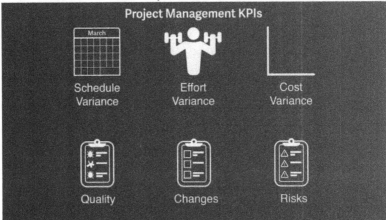

For projects we can see this typical list of KPIs that show whether you're hitting your objectives and key results or critical success factors. We can see several from schedule variance to effort variance and cost variance. We take a look at the quality the number of changes that are identified implemented or rejected. These are all ways to measure the success of whether something is working within projects. By the way that is true of whether it's an Agile project or a traditional waterfall - more of a predictive type of project. For Service Management we can see that there are a lot of different things. In fact a bigger influence of things like TCO or Total Cost of Ownership, operational and standard service level agreements. You've got performance and availability. This is where you start hearing things like five nines uptime. You hear terms like meantime between failure and meantime to restore service. Or perhaps number of feature releases and upgrades that might happen there. All of those things as KPIs for Service Management tie into much more of a day to day operational type of environment, versus projects which typically are going to be what we started here, we're doing things here and eventually there is an end game that we want to accomplish, the requirements that our customers or even within our own organization is looking for. But what would this look like if I wanted to continue on in a career perhaps is being a project Manager? Are there some differences? Well here we see a generalized path from being a project coordinator which simply requires a high school diploma or equivalent secondary education.

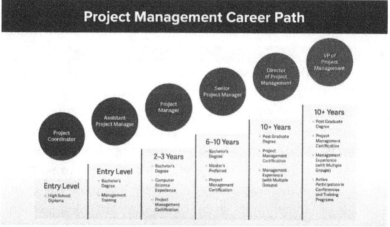

Here in the States we would say something like a GED or a General Education Document. This can climb up to ultimately being the Vice President of Project Management at a major company. The nice thing here is how high you go is only limited by your willingness to continue learning proper Project Management skills and doing as many projects and doing them well as possible. For IT Service Management, there are way more roles and positions that you see. But the ones that we are showing are broken down into fairly typical what we call the three point areas. Strategic, Developmental - sometimes called Tactical and Operational.

Common Careers in IT Service Management

Strategic	Development	Operations
○ Service Level Manager	○ Release Manager	○ Service Desk Technician
○ IT Architect	○ Change Manager	○ Security Analyst
○ Security Architect	○ Configuration Manager	○ Incident Manager
○ Cyber Resilience Consultant		○ IT Operations Manager

To get to these positions, we do a lot of things from education to experience. We can see everything from strategic type of roles or a service level Manager creating those service level agreements to security architects IT architects. You can move into something that's more of a developmental type of thing. Whether you're into software or application development and that's going to be things like Change Management and Configuration Management, Release and Deployment Management positions and then Operations. Those are the parts that a lot of times when you're getting your start in IT, this is where you show up. You're going to be on the Service Desk. Maybe helping out with Incident Management maybe being the IT Operations Manager as you move up along that particular path. Not only with Project Management and IT Service Management, education and Certification can be your friend. So let's start off with something in the realm of Project Management.

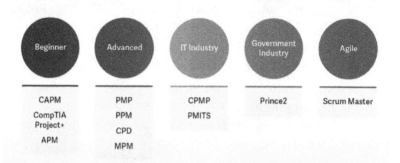

Project Management Certifications

Beginner	Advanced	IT Industry	Government Industry	Agile
CAPM	PMP	CPMP	Prince2	Scrum Master
CompTIA Project+	PPM	PMITS		
APM	CPD			
	MPM			

These Project Management Certifications I'm just showing you a small list of some of them that are available. These are probably some of the more well known ones and I will be the first to say that you don't need to hold Certification in order to get some of those positions that we were talking about, whether it was Project Management or whether it was IT Service Management. But definitely will help you with career advancement and with more money. So let's first look at these Project Management certs and we can see that we have everything if you're looking at it from a level, we can start over there on the left with the beginner levels of CAPM, which is the Certified Associate of a Project Management. CompTia is Project Plus. There's also IT Project Management and APM which is another one. Then we have advanced which is going to be something like a PMP which is a Project Management Professional. I will warn you that some of these certs in the advanced areas more than likely will require some Project Management experience. Just for example the PMP requires at a minimum if you have a four year university degree or graduate level degree, you need 4500 hours of Project Management experience. There's the PMP, there's the PPM which is just another different way of looking at things. CPD MPM or Managing Projects Master and then we have different types of industries. You've got the IT Industry which would be the CPMP, the Project Management IT Services and these are also great Certifications. If you're in the government and that type of industry the Prince2 which comes from Axelos which is also the same organization that produces ITIL which is an IT Service Management Certification. These are really good because they were developed by the UK government. Prince2 kind of came out of that. Then Agile one that's very well known there are more but Scrum Master or Certified Scrum Master is a great Certification to grab if you are into that Agile type of Project Management. Let's take a look at IT Service Management as well. The one that I'm going to show is the one I'm most familiar with. There are others here that we have. Things like COBIT there is Siam and there is VeriSM but let's move on to ITIL.

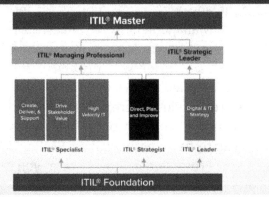

ITIL stands for Information Technology Infrastructure Library. It is probably the most well known IT Service Management Certification System out there. It's been around for 30 plus years and it is one that is recognized worldwide. You can find these ITIL managing Professionals and Strategic Leaders all over the globe. You can start off with something as simple as an ITIL 4 Foundation and you can go out take an exam in your ITIL 4 Foundation certified. From there you can move up into those middle and almost intermediate level type Certifications which can be just if you want to do one or a couple there are ones that are just for you. You can do anything from the create deliver and support, drive stakeholder value. There's high velocity IT and then one that works both for the ITIL for managing Professional and Strategic Leader is something called Direct Plan & Improve which deals with how do you create those improvement initiatives. How do you take your organization higher? Then something that has just been released something called the ITIL for Strategic Leader in which case you can take the ITIL Leader Certification which is digital in IT Strategy. If you get both ITIL for Management Professional and the ITIL for Strategic Leader you have the option to become an ITIL Master. There are very very few ITIL Masters in the world and it's kind of like having your PhD in IT Service Management. Well there you have it. A detailed look at the differences between Project and Service Management as well as if maybe you're looking for some Certification.

Chapter 19 Service Operations Management and ITSM

With the age of Technology we live in today no business can do without ITSM. A discipline that is used to manage small, medium and large-scale it systems in a business or organization, you would definitely be surprised at the massive impact a fully integrated ITSM system can have on your business. In fact in a market report named global ITSM market 2020 to 2024 generated by Technavio, it is stated that the IT Service Management market size is expected to grow by 3.29 billion us dollars during 2020 to 2024. The report also states that the advent of technologies such as machine learning, blockchain, big data, artificial intelligence IoT and virtual reality will increase the adoption of advanced ITSM solutions by enterprises. First we are going to introduce ITSM to you starting with one of the stages of the ITIL library which is called service Operations and then we're going to go into what that particular stage does in supporting IT Service Management. Then we'll go into IT Service Management as a whole. Let's get started with revisiting some of the Foundation Information you may have learned in your ITIL Foundation. The basic five stages of the Information Technology Infrastructure Library Service Lifecycle Framework includes having a strategy around what services your business plans to offer supported by your underpinning IT organization. Then designing IT Services which includes what your architects and engineers do. Then transitioning services from a pre-deployment pre-development mode pre-production mode into the production environment by releasing deployment, Change Management, Knowledge Management and so on of the additional processes. Service operation is a very critical stage because that's where we say the value of IT Services is seen by users and customers. That's what we consider the factory of IT and that's where we measure where users are maybe unhappy with our service or they're extremely happy with our service. Surrounding all of the other four stages is continual service improvement and that's where we conduct quality assurance and quality control. That's just a little background around the ITIL Service lifecycle and where we are today with the framework. Concentrating on one stage particularly is service operation. It consists of five processes; Event Management, Incident Management, Request Fulfillment, Access Management and Problem Management. The four functional areas include the Service Desk, IT Operations Management, Application Management and Technical Management. All of those areas are needed to support delivering IT Services and operating IT Services. It's a collaborative effort between standardized reputable processes and functional teams and people which are called functions. This particular stage of the ITIL life cycle is a very important stage because that's where we carry out day-to-day tasks and activities. Those day-to-day activities are used to deliver services at agreed service levels. What are agreed service levels? Service level requirements that are documented and service level agreements. This is also the stage that is responsible for ongoing Management of Technology used to deliver services, support services, maintain stability of services and also improve services to the CSI team. There are stages and underneath the stages there are processes and functions. Service Management as a practice means that you are using a capability around managing IT Services to keep your services at a quality functional level that you have agreed to in service level agreements. The service life cycle is an approach that takes all five stages together; strategy, design, transition, Ops and CSI in support of delivering quality IT Services. All of those stages together is known as the Service Management life cycle. How you operate the life cycle is called ITSM or Managing Services. In order to manage IT Services you have to understand what your business goals are which are called business requirements. Business requirements are identified in the service strategy stage. It is beneficial for every CIO to communicate to all of its IT staff what is the business mission, business goals, business objectives, sustainability for the company as a whole and then identify your IT strategy. We always start with a business strategy. We communicate that down to an IT strategy and then we design, transition, operate and improve. The five operational processes include managing events - that's event correlation by using tools in the infrastructure in the enterprise to notify desktops, laptops, email and mobile phones of activity within your infrastructure managing Incidents. Incidents are tickets that you take at the Service Desk. Those tickets can be emails, they can be phone calls, they can be text messages and they can be IMs. Incident Management is at the core of Operations because this tells you how your users are operating around the services that you're providing. If they're unhappy with those services they will log in and ticket. Managing problems are not Incidents and problems is where you get to the root core - to the root reason why that Incident took place. This is where we conduct root cause analysis. Managing requests; this is where we identify standardized low-level tickets by folks calling in around an issue around maybe their desktop or maybe their laptop or maybe it's a password reset but it's not a problem or an Incident. Access Management is more about granting access to IT Services from users around using IT Services and a lot of organizations refer to access Management as Identity Management. Processes have a beginning and an end. Processes have inputs and outputs. Processes exist to accomplish a specific objective. Under the service operation stage there are five processes; repeatable standardized measurable processes that every organization should try to stand up if you're going to follow ITIL best practices to manage your infrastructure environments. Service operation functions are functional areas of teams. Teams are groups of people. There are four major teams in the ITIL best practice framework that carry out the five processes. Those teams include the Service Desk. We used to call the Service Desk the Help desk. The Service Desk is able to take Incident tickets and Service Requests. The Technical Management team that manages designers, architects and engineers and they maintain the mainframe servers, network, storage, database, directory services, desktop middleware and the internet. IT Operations is the team that sits in the network Operations center and they manage day-to-day activities and they handle backups and restore and also manage facilities. Application Management is the functional Operations team that handles any tickets around software, business applications and any in-house applications that have been raised. They can also be handled by application service providers as well.

Chapter 20 IT Operations Functions

What happens in IT Operations function itself? Well, this is where we concentrate on maintaining stability of the organization services and this is where we will route and escalate tickets to the folks that sit in the network area that sit in the NOC or the Network Operations Center or the Data Center and they take tickets as well but they're handling more real-time issues and Incidents that come through the Service Desk, versus technical Management and those are the folks that manage long-term engineering efforts. A lot of organizations will not re-org just to support delivery of IT Services so this is a suggestion out of the ITIL library that you should understand what services you offer, how many services you offer, what those services do, who your customers are and you should figure out what teams and process areas and functional areas support those services. That way we can maintain business satisfaction and confidence to our customers and users that rely on those services. We know how to manage those services to reduce outages and failures and we know how to operate those services if the business is impacted by any of those services on a day-to-day basis. We want to understand what we offer, who supports those services, why we offer those services and how those services provide value. We know that services are intangible and they're hard to measure, but it's really important to understand which services are critical, admission critical and vital to the business so that we can maintain stability. Remember that Operations is where users and customers come in contact with our services and that's why we say Operations is the area where actual value is seen. How do we deliver and manage IT Services? Well first of all we need to understand what is a service. Going back to our ITIL Foundation course services are a means of delivering value to customers by helping customers facilitate outcomes.

Customers don't own services - they use services. Service providers own services and our job as a provider is to facilitate outcomes by enhancing performances and reducing constraints and risk, and mitigating issues. We own the services, we minimize the risk but we deliver a service that enhances the performance of some type of outcome a user or customer is trying to fulfil. So our job is to enable - we are an enabler. Some of our services include email, hosting, backup, print services, storage services, hosting services, cloud services and all services are intangibles. The Technology that sits under services include the physical environment, the tangible part of IT but services themselves are intangible that's why they're so hard to manage. How we manage the performance of a service is all wrapped around service level agreements or SLAs. You cannot manage a service unless you know what the expectations are, the uptime, the maintenance time and what will happen to our customers if a service goes down. Will there be any penalties involved because you inconvenienced your users? Our job in managing services effectively and efficiently, is to make sure that reduce service costs improve stability, improve overall performance and continue to optimize that service so that the business can sustain its vision mission and objectives in the future. With understanding that, operating services is just a part of delivering quality services. The whole big picture and the holistic view of everything we do around IT is referred to as ITSM or Information Technology Service Management. It does not represent supplier Management or substituting the S for anything else except for Service Management. It's been around for over 20 years. ITIL came out in the 80s so it's not new, it's not a trend and it's not a fad. Service Management is where the business interfaces with the technical teams and everybody understands hearing the message from the CIO at the same time what our business does and what our services deliver and how the IT department supports those services and what the business needs to do to sustain its Operations in the future ongoing by making sure that we collaborate with people, steps and processes, products and tools, partners, vendors, third parties, suppliers and providers. Everybody needs to hear that message at the same time from our CIO by having some type of all hands meeting or regular brown bag meetings that the business as a whole is taking on the approach of ITSM by integrating with our underpinning IT teams. It's not just about Technology and it's not just about ROI and making money. It's everything that we do in the entire IT organization to make sure that IT systems underpin business services. So you need to understand what are your business services that make you money and what are your IT Services. Those are two different things but ITSM brings those two areas together. SM or Service Management includes everything that it organization does to keep services up and running. That means documenting, sharing knowledge, standing up Technology, communicating, knowledge Management, interfacing with our vendors, contracts and that mean service level agreements. So ITSM is an organizational-wide approach to delivering services and supporting services an organizational-wide approach. That means anything that IT does we're going to bring the business executives in line with our goals and objectives. Anything that the business does that involves IT they're going to invite IT to those meetings and all C level executives and IT representatives are going to come to the same page and sharing outcomes, objectives and expectations. They're going to agree and they're going to sign on the dotted line and we do not do any of our work in silos. So it is a holistic approach and it's great to bring in our business partners and our providers and suppliers as well so they understand we are using a best practice approach to managing IT. But why do we need ITSM? What does it do for us? Well it makes sure that the IT folks understand what the business is doing and the business side of the house understands what the IT department is doing so it's an inclusive view of managing the entire enterprise and the infrastructure.

We're not going to work and siloed teams in a mushroom without understanding what the executives do, without understanding what our Incident representatives do at the Incident Management desk. It is an organizational wide approach, so ITSM is in need because there is increased dependency on delivering IT Services. Delivering IT Service s needs a collaborative approach. We need business executives on board, we need external suppliers to do their job and we need an internal technical view and all combined is what is made up of an IT Service Management approach. If there is any failure at all in IT that means that customers know about it, users know about it and service failures are very visible and the business may take a hit. So it's very inclusive to understand that everybody has a role and everybody has a responsibility in making sure that IT Services are always up and running and available when needed and we can't place blame on others. It's all of our fault if an IT Service experiences a failure. Most organizations are increasing the complexity of the infrastructure so everyone has to be involved at the same time and hear the messages, have access to the documents, share Information better and communicate better because expectations are higher of us as individuals as analysts as IT staff and customers have higher expectations, the market itself is changing, the IT industry is changing too so we all need to understand our approach to managing services by documenting what our IT Service Management approach is going to be. Changes also take place all the time so we have to know how to manage change and this is not new. This has been around for a while. Businesses are starting to charge for IT Services. In the past when you used email, email used to be free. Email is being charged for now. Google charges for email. When you used to fly in an airplane, we used to get pillows and blankets and food for free. Now all of those services we are charging for food, we are charging for a better seat and what we thought was free in the past is now um becoming an expense so we need to know how to manage that better on how we can expand our profits and make sure that we are charging for our services appropriately. Some of the goals of ITSM include improving the quality of the services we are providing and that goes in line with sometimes understanding that services are not free. IT is not free. IT has a lot of expenses and sometimes we have to roll those expenses over onto our customers. We need a good Professional approach to managing IT and we need to make sure our customers are always satisfied because our company is being compared to other companies. We need to make sure the morale with our staff they're always motivated and they are enthusiastic about their jobs. If you have a service environment where you're always impacted by failures and outages, then the morale of your staff goes down, so we need to talk about how ITSM can help us with managing a motivated staff. Talking about money and cost and maintaining profit and managing our businesses so we have sustainability, we do nothing in ITSM without understanding that everything has a dollar sign attached to it. We need to manage what our budgets are and we need to account for IT cost and we need to have an IT budget. Aligning IT Services to understanding what the business goals are is very important. The business and the IT department need to be in the same car, same road, same lane not having conflict, so we need to have clear idea of what our capabilities are what our strengths and weaknesses, our opportunities, our threats are, our external threats our internal vulnerabilities. We always need to know what our customer needs are. We need to document our business plans and then we need to supplement business plans with IT strategic plans. We have business plans and we have IT Service plans. For example if you think about a bank ATM screen you touch buttons. Those buttons are services. We see those buttons as customers but internally those are business services and behind business services there are IT Services. We need to make the experience for the business users better by ramping up our IT Services, so IT Services underpinned business services and every single button you touch on an ATM screen is considered a business service that is supported by Infrastructure Technology. So the practice of understanding Service Management is that we have an organizational wide view. It's not an internal technical view. We are getting out of our bubbles out of our mushrooms out of our silos we are lining up with the goals of the business and we are linking our individual jobs with what the business wants to succeed in as a whole. Interlocking IT Service Management disciplines will allow the needs of the customer to be matched by the capability of the IT Services being offered. IT Services support business goals and objectives. We're going to follow best practices and use the ITIL approach to understanding the entire environment by bringing together business executives and IT technical staff so that we can manage the performance of IT Services better and offer more quality IT Services that never go down. IT Services need to be up and running 24 hours a day seven days a week and that's tough to do. It's not always when we have a maintenance window that we can work in and services can go down while we work on them and then users will wait until that service comes back up - that's not the case. We need to operate and maintain services in the background, but users never want to log out. That's tough to do so the name of the game is availability, and providing quality services. How do we provide quality services? We have an ITSM approach. We document a strategy how we're going to design our services, we transition them, we operate them and we improve them so it's an organizational perspective. We don't do anything in IT that the business wouldn't support and the business will communicate with the IT organization if they're going down the right lane in their strategic approach. The importance of ITSM is that organizations want to make money and if they don't want to make money if they're not for profit, they want to please their constituents, their customers and their users. How do we do that? We are able to show that IT Services have value attached to them by measuring what our services do. Once we can show and prove and justify and quantify the value of IT, we can sustain our business and we can grow our customers and we can expand our business into other markets. So by strategizing, designing, transitioning, operating and improving, we can do the following. Expand what we do as a company, adapt to market changes and industry changes, increase our revenues and profits, reduce our penalties when there are any service outages, service more customers and expand our base and expand the users we are supporting, prevent loss, be more proactive, have more preventative measures in place and create loyalty, confidence and trust. We do that by understanding what we're good at, our strengths, our weaknesses, our opportunities, our threats and our resources. What our capabilities are creating IT Services, creating value in IT Services, measuring the uptime our services offer, delivering services to users and customers and that's how we fulfill business outcomes. It's a whole enterprise organizational-wide effort and it takes everyone involved to make sure that our businesses is successful at the end of the day.

Chapter 21 Interfaces within ITSM

The interfaces between the different functional teams and the processes are very important because we have to understand what other process areas support and what other functional areas do so we can operate as a fine-tuned machine. We can operate as an orchestra, a symphony where everybody has a rule and we are taking a holistic approach to supporting IT Service initiatives and IT Service projects. Just like a football team has many parts involved to win a game, it takes the coaches, the staff, it takes the players, it's a whole group effort and every member has a part to play and that's what ITSM is about - a holistic approach. ITSM projects are supported by IT Operations functions and design engineers and CSI staff and Change Management staff and problem Managers and DevOps. Everybody is part of this machine. For example managing changes, managing configuration updates, release and deployment. We all have to understand how we all contribute and how one activity affects another and how one team affects the business and making sure that our service level agreements are adhered to. At the end of the day service level agreements are how we promote the value of IT Services. We measure what we do, we capture when services are up, we capture when services are down, we create reports and those reports are communicated up to business executives, business executives interface with paying customers and we promote our successful performance activities on our websites and that's how we gain new business. Sometimes we do get business from folks just kind of randomly surfing and discovering our business and what we do by looking at our business metrics. Those business metrics need to be positive at all time, especially if your environment operates 24x7 and some of your IT metrics include 99.999% availability, you have to meet five nines. You have to do better than your competitors because we're always being measured. So because we're always being measured, that includes interfacing with all our other teammates, all our other functional groups and all of our other process areas. Managing services via ITSM means that we understand what our individual jobs and roles contribute to the business as a whole and how our outsourcers, our partners, third party, vendors and external suppliers interface with us. Our external parties need to understand what ITSM is as well. You have cloud service providers, application service providers, you have internet service providers and you don't want to place blame when one of our providers bring something down and you say that's out of our hands because the customers only are interfacing with you. They don't even know about your underpinning providers, so we want to understand what everyone does, how everyone contributes to the environment, how we can reduce service outages by communicating well across external parties. With ITSM at the forefront, we know that it's a collaborative effort that managing Incidents, root cause analysis and Problem Management, Continuity Management, external vendor a supplier Management, managing and governance around policies, procedures, work instructions, standard operating procedures and processes - all need to be documented and they all need to be shared, even amongst our partners and even amongst our contractors or our vendors and our consultants so that we understand who does what and how we can all contribute to making our services more reliable and more available.

Chapter 22 The Value of ITSM

The value that ITSM provides is that we want to make sure that we can measure our work. Providing services is very tough and very complex and services are intangible but at the end of the day, you cannot measure what you don't know how to manage. So we need to be able to document what we're doing, how fast, when we have outages, when customers maybe are complaining, how many tickets we're logging, how much money we're charging - all of that is under Service Management. Everything that we do is valued by the business and every stakeholder is a contributor. Technology is managed by many different parts and pieces and improvements need to be documented. Perception is important because if we have a service that's constantly up and down up and down up and down and the perception is that service is poor, well that customer doesn't want to do business with us anymore, and that means that we're going to lose business. So all of that comes into play under ITSM; exceptions, expectations, perception, reputation, surveys, how we interact with vendors - a holistic business-wide organizational approach and documenting our successes and promoting our successes as well. Support teams of the infrastructure will need to align around IT and you need to promote and document and quantify everything that you've done to keep that service up and available and reliable for customers to use according to their SLAs. Measuring services extremely important because you cannot manage what you don't measure. You cannot measure what you don't manage, so it's about control and it's about managing risk and it's about being proactive and measuring what your services are doing to support business applications and how your services are helping to keep the company successful. All services need to be measured every single day, all day long as long as they're up and running within your service level agreement and that's how we consider controlling risk. Managing internal vulnerabilities and managing external threats. It's really important that you use different types of controls to manage your environment. Automation is very important but we also have some manual controls as well; continuous monitoring tools, event Management tools, event correlation. Understanding what services are critical, what services are major, what services are significant, what services are minor and communicating what those services are to our partners and understanding when our number one customer calls and how we service them and what our hours of service are during the day. Are we are 24 by seven, 23 by seven, nine to five or nine to six and what that looks like do we have any automatic self-healing utilities that are operational so that we can see what's going on 24x7 and if we need manual activities to come into play, we can use our event correlation tools to give us a heads up and bring in our human beings to support the environment as well. All activities are measured whether they are automatic or manual.

Chapter 23 Maintenance of IT Services

Maintenance of IT Services is very important because we don't want to be a reactive environment. We do want to be proactive. It is very important to try to see an event happening in your environment before a user calls. That represents the quality of IT so that needs to be communicated to external vendors as well. Testing it systems is extremely important. This happens before you go live. This happens pre-production and we do this in the design and transition stage of the idle life cycle. Diagnostic tools are very important. Identifying known errors, common workarounds that needs to be communicated to the Operations team and the Incident Management team at the Service Desk. Documenting lessons learned via knowledge Management systems if you're using something like SharePoint that's very important so we can see past performance and we can see historical Information. We can communicate amongst different shifts within the teams and we can identify whether a tool should be continually used or maybe we should stop using a specific tool. Improvement activities need to be documented as well. Setting triggers, thresholds - this is all a part of ITSM and Management of IT Services. ITSM is everything that you do and everything that you manage and everything that you document and your communication and your automation and event correlation - it's everything that you do and understanding how you carry out those activities. We have an interface between Service Management and interfacing with external vendors suppliers and providers as well. In a lot of publications you will see that providers are more in-house and suppliers are more external, but no company manages IT without best practices being considered, and best practices is where we rely on the ITIL library and within the ITIL library is where we get our ITSM approach. We see companies like Procter & Gamble, Disney, Microsoft, DHL and many others rely on ITSM to improve their IT organizations. Services are now expanding into infrastructure as a Service, Desktop as a service, software as a service and many systems that have been internal to organizations are now being operated in the cloud and as environments become more complex, it will be more clear to understanding what ITSM can do for us to manage services that are internal to our organizations and services that are being managed by external companies as well. It is a coordinated effort amongst internal staff and external providers as well. We need to have a good strategy, we need to have a good IT strategic plan, we need to be flexible to changes, we need to have coordinated efforts in play, so ITSM is where we overlap with our service providers. We explain to them what our strategic plans are and we have them sign up within service level agreements and vendor contracts that they do understand what our ITSM practices are, so everybody is on the same page and we have a business perspective and play and we have governing policies overarching our work and we have service level agreements that we have to adhere to and we have ITSM strategic plans that we communicate to internal staff and external vendors as well. This is how we maintain high customer satisfaction and high customer confidence. When you're interfacing with service suppliers whether they be a strategic supplier or a commodity supplier, maybe they're providing electricity or maintenance or storage support or application development support, we need to understand what our suppliers do for us and how often they respond to events or if they are coming to our facility, how those contracts read and how available those suppliers are to us in supporting IT Services that they own but they help to manage. You need to have clear lines drawn as to who owns what services and who manages. There is a big difference between owning a service and just managing a service. This process area is referred to as Supplier Management and that's under ITSM as well.

Chapter 24 Supplier Management Objectives

Suppliers can be categorized into different areas around the support that they provide to us. There can be strategic suppliers like internet service providers. There can be operational suppliers like cloud suppliers there can be tactical suppliers - suppliers that provide services email. There can be commodity suppliers that supply electricity or gas or heat or backups, so you need to know what your vendors do, do they understand our best practice approach, what their response levels are, what they're being charged, what the penalties are and it's really important that you regularly meet with your vendors so they understand that your company is implementing a best practice approach. There is a great correlation and collaboration between operating, managing services and having some of that Management activity supported by external vendors. We call external vendors suppliers. You may call them providers as well, but you want to be clear as who is doing what. There are definitions for strategic suppliers and these are the folks that are doing more designing and architecture and engineering work, long term strategic planning, more work that impacts our company as a whole and there are tactical vendors that do more middle Management more day-to-day work for us as well and they need to be readily available when our services are impacted. There are operational vendors that manage day-to-day activities. For example you may outsource your entire Service Desk. You may outsource your entire HR department and that's fine. That's an operational vendor for you and that should seem seamless. It shouldn't seem as if you are outsourcing it and you're always placing blame on this external vendor. It should be that they are a partner and part of your environment and you work very closely together and you shouldn't be pointing fingers. We depend on commodity vendors for some of the physical and tangible work that they do for us but we shouldn't port them out as they are external to our business. They're very important to our business and they're also a partner that impact how our services are provided as well. Maintaining stability is the name of the game when you are managing services. It should seem seamless no matter how many vendors you interface with and no matter how many suppliers and partners, contractors or consultants you interface with. It should all seem very seamless because we all understand our ITSM organizational-wide approach, we understand why the business exists, we understand the services that we offer and we understand our individual role and responsibilities. That means that the quality of the service is very important to everyone involved, meeting those service level agreements and meeting business expectations is at the forefront of everything that we do. We leverage our work amongst each other across teams and across departments and across divisions. We follow policy and the business is our governing body so what the business says goes. What services impact the business is what we pay attention to and put those in the top 10 or the top three list of systems that we need to make sure are up and running at all times, and that's what we call when we conduct a business impact analysis. Understanding what services are extremely important to the business and then those services are the ones that we need to make sure in the IT organization we keep viable and sustainable and available and reliable to users and customers at all times. Everyone has a role - we are all a part of this well-oiled machine. The business and the IT department and our vendors all working together all at the same time. In conclusion I want to make sure that everyone totally understood that this organizational-wide perspective is integrating more business activity with IT and managing partner, relationships Technology implementations, enabling people to be well skilled to be informed to be knowledgeable to share Information and to document our standardized repeatable processes to have a good strategy that we support, we are in alignment with the business and the business is in alignment with our IT organization. Our ITSM approach is that we understand how the business wants us to operate, we are an underpinning organization to the business and we collaborate together, even with our partners and we understand how services contribute to providing value to our customers. We also do not point fingers, we do not work in silos, we want our customers to come to us and not go straight to our vendor and in fact they don't even need to know that we are using vendors for different things because we're going to make the environment so seamless to them. Remember that manage IT Services from an enterprise perspective include governance and policy at the forefront. Make sure you understand what the business mission goals and objectives are, communicate that down to the IT department and make sure the IT department clearly communicates with all of its staff with good processes, documented good procedures, automation clearly understood by everyone and we have a good working relationship with our suppliers and vendors as well and that way our services can always be reliable a hundred percent of the time. It's important to make sure that our environments environment maintains stability and we minimize risk and we have a little bit more control in our environment as well.

Chapter 25 COBIT VS ITIL

IT organizations commonly utilize frameworks for IT Service Management called ITSM however companies utilizing only one of these frameworks are missing out on significant benefits. In fact the majority of available ITSM best practice bodies are designed to co-exist with other frameworks, offering complementary features and capabilities. These include COBIT 2019 and ITIL 4. ITIL is the most popular service Management framework worldwide. COBIT is recognized globally for enterprise governance and IT Management. Each framework is highly effective in providing customized governance and quality service Management, however when combined COBIT and ITIL have the potential to increase the value significantly, not only for the customer but for the entire organization and its partners as well. Therefore the question remains. What are the differences between COBIT and ITIL and how should they be utilized in conjunction? So in this chapter let's look at the differences between these two ITSM concepts. Initially we shall brush up on the two main terminologies ITIL al and COBIT then we shall focus on the main topic that is the differences between ITIL and COBIT. Then we shall see which ITSM methodology is better for you. IT Service Management refers to how technical teams design plan and implement daily it procedures for their clients and businesses. As technology continues to play a central role in businesses, organizations must find creative ways to incorporate IT Services into their daily operations. ITSM is all about developing a process-driven approach to IT Services, as opposed to traditional tech-driven IT Management approaches. As a result, it focuses on the customer's needs rather than traditional IT Services. In other words, unlike the majority of IT Management practices which tend to focus on internal hardware, networks and systems, ITSM utilizes IT Services to bridge the gap between customer service and business objectives. Since its introduction in the 1980s when it was primarily used for data center Management, ITSM has undergone significant development. In the past it merely provided a structured method for managing IT resources. Modern ITSM encompasses all encompassing business and IT convergence best practices. There is a good thing that you have already implemented some ITSM processes in your organization however as your organization expands you will need to implement more mature processes to maximize the return on your ITSM investments. Now we shall discuss what is COBIT. COBIT is essentially a methodology that focuses on aligning business and IT objectives. It simply assigns responsibilities and goals to business and IT managers to streamline their processes. COBIT provides all the tools necessary to construct, monitor and enhance its implementation while reducing costs and establishing and preserving privacy standards. To simply put, COBIT provides structure and oversight for general IT processes within an organization. COBIT includes numerous resources such as frameworks, process descriptions, control objectives, Management guidelines and maturity models that can facilitate the Management and governance of an IT organization. The COBIT framework is entirely based on the guiding principles of meeting stakeholder needs, comprehensive protection of the enterprise, organizations using a single integrated framework, developing or initiating a holistic strategy differentiating governance from organization or Management. But what is ITIL? ITIL is a framework for service Management that provides enterprises with guidance on how to use it for business development transformation and change. ITIL 4 continues to provide organizations with the guidance they need to address new service Management challenges and how to use different technology in the era of DevOps, Agile, Cloud and Digital Transformation. The key components of the ITIL 4 framework represent a significant evolution from previous versions of ITIL.

After understanding both the concepts we shall see the difference between COBIT and ITIL. ITIL applies governance to provide value to all stakeholders whereas COBIT attempts to govern all organizational processes. Similar aspects of the ITILv3 service life cycle are apparent when examining each framework however we must recognize that the expected outcomes are distinct. COBIT seeks end-to-end governance while ITILv4 seeks to create business value. Still, they can co-exist. These frameworks may be combined by an organization to govern the environment users and stakeholders may be confused so only highly mature organizations with mature processes practices should consider the possibility. Due to the fact that each framework has its own list of processes albeit with significant overlap, an organization may use the best of breed to achieve the best results. COBIT is significantly more robust in areas such as supplier Management, continuity and security among others. ITIL 4 and ITILv3 are also superior in areas that ITIL 4 refers to as general Management practices such as strategy Management, architecture Management, service financial Management, Workforce and Talent Management, continual improvement organizational change Management and relationship Management. Both frameworks are robust in conventional control areas change Management, configuration Management and asset Management. COBIT is more important in areas where ITIL 4 lacks control, whereas ITIL 4 is more robust in areas requiring collaboration with stakeholders particularly the business. Neither ITIL 4 nor COBIT should be mandated for a specific organization. Instead, documented requirements with clearly defined objectives and outcomes should be mapped to the application framework. The most important question is which framework should be used? COBIT and ITIL are undeniably two of the best ITSM tools available, however we can simply state that COBIT's coverage is broader than ITILs. By definition ISACA's covet is a framework for developing, monitoring, implementing and improving information technology governance and Management. COBIT stands for Control Objectives for Information and Related Technology Information Systems Audit and Control Association. COBIT's primary objective is to provide a common language for executives to communicate rules, objectives, requirements, goals and outcomes. ITIL which stands for Information Technology Infrastructure Library is a framework consisting of a collection of best practices, planning and selection that focuses on enhancing IT Services in accordance with business requirements. ITIL is also defined as a set of procedures for enhancing and enhancing the IT Service lifecycle. 2019 marks the release of the latest version of ITIL which includes best practices for IT Services. COBIT and ITIL almost cover the same area of work and IT professionals have utilized them for years in ITSM. COBIT and ITIL can provide enterprises with governance and Management guidance, however it would not be incorrect to assert that COBIT's scope is much broader than that of an ITSM system. The COBIT approach to ITSM is a top-down approach that differentiates between the Management and governance of IT Services from a business perspective. COBIT more closely resembles the application of strategy to governance and Management. It is only concerned with governance. ITIL's approach to ITSM is more likely a bottom-up approach from an IT business model perspective. ITIL focuses primarily on tactics and ITSM focuses primarily on the Management of IT Services. The goals of COBIT is to manage the IT department for the company's benefit and steer it in the right direction, align IT goals with business objectives, bring IT benefits to the organization, manage IT efficiency, risks and resources. On the other hand ITIL's goals are to ensure the organization's IT Services are organized and running smoothly, create possibilities for continuous operational excellence, reduce the organization's IT expenses without sacrificing efficiency, enhanced decision making within the organization. COBIT effectively addresses the general problems for instance if a system frequently fails audits COBIT provides a set of benchmarks for audits that evaluate the IT system by using them frequently for internal audits and becoming partners for the external audit of IT systems. ITIL effectively addresses general issues. For instance if IT teams are constantly overworked, ITIL provides service transition and operation for IT departments in detail according to various IT Services, drastically reducing downtime costs. Control objectives, maturity models, Management guidelines, process descriptions and a framework are fundamental COBIT components. ITIL's fundamental elements include service strategy, service design, service transition, service operation and continuous service improvement, also known as the five ITIL principles. The certification aids individuals as a knowledge base in Service Management and ultimately the organization and its Management of IT Services. The certification assists individuals in advancing their careers by enabling them to perform IT governance roles and ultimately by enhancing customer satisfaction within the organization. But can COBIT and ITIL coexist? COBIT provides the what, whereas ITIL demonstrates the how. However their most recent iterations continue to complement one another. Both concepts focus on how to convert stakeholder desires into value and are custom-made for the organization. This customization enables businesses to utilize the most advantageous parts and how they need them. Let's look at some examples. ITIL 4 places a greater emphasis on governance than previous versions, devoting an entire SVS ring to it. This enables businesses to comprehend better how and where COBIT fits into their strategy. ITIL 4 also provides detailed guidance on how to implement several COBIT processes. Change Management is one example where ITIL defines a structure and a process for executing this practice correctly. This structure can also help ITIL using organizations continue to derive real value from their IT capabilities while simultaneously avoiding risks. COBIT 2019 will create

Management objectives and governance directly based on the needs of stakeholders. ITIL 4 will guide these specific needs through its service value system, transforming inputs into valuable outputs for customers and the business. COBIT 2019 employs gold cascading - a visual waterfall that cascades from stakeholder need to enterprise goals to assist organizations in meeting their stakeholders needs. This mechanism improves ITIL efficacy and supports Service Management by prioritizing ITSM improvement opportunities, identifying essential IT Service Management and ITSM activities, improvement proposals by tying them to specific organizational goals. But where do ITIL and COBIT intersect? COBIT and ITIL share a nearly identical scope of application, making it difficult to choose between them. Furthermore, numerous processes correspond between the two platforms such as the BAI06 managing changes process and COBIT in the ITIL change Management process. In addition, ITIL does not contain a specific risk Management process, whereas COBIT includes the risk Management process. Thus it is evident that there is some overlap between these platforms and you must keep in mind that if COBIT functions as an antibiotic, then ITIL will function as an antipyretic. Both of these concepts play a significant role in IT Service Management and have complementary but distinct objectives. Developers are continually attempting to enhance ITIL's approach to development. In simpler terms, we can say there is no alternative to ITIL whereas there are multiple alternatives to COBIT. For example COBIT is typically used for auditing functions in enterprise IT, whereas ITIL is utilized for process improvement. Therefore as the IT Management department of an enterprise, we recommend combining both of these platforms rather than selecting only one. Finally we shall see ITIL versus COBIT or ITIL and COBIT? Evidently, these two work closely together and generally have the same goal, making IT stable and efficient. However this does not imply that this is the only way they look good. ITIL and COBIT function quite well independently. You may find it odd to employ a tactic ITIL without a strategy, COBIT however it should not be forgotten that ITIL also provides strategic fundamentals for IT Services organizations which are sufficient for the early stages. Moreover, based on the differences in their approaches, definitions and most importantly objectives, COBIT appears to be more suited for large IT mature businesses. It requires a large number of IT processes and an extensive IT infrastructure to govern. While ITIL can be a good starting point for achieving such scope in general and a high level of IT maturity in particular, it is insufficient. If you're deciding between COBIT versus ITIL, the decision is straightforward. The first phase of your ITSM implementation project should likely involve ITIL, and once you have mastered its intricacies, you can begin to think more globally using COBIT. But which ITSM framework is right for you? When comparing COBIT and ITIL, neither replaces the other. Numerous businesses use both. COBIT aligns IT goals with business objectives and ensures maximum value and minimum risk from IT resources. ITIL is used to design, develop and improve an IT Service that is efficient, effective and supportive of business initiatives and needs. Therefore should your company use both? That depends. ITIL and COBIT can be useful for very large or highly regulated organizations that require a strong focus on governance. This belt and braces approach to ITSM ensures that IT resources are allocated consistently and in accordance with the organization's objectives, however the COBIT vs ITIL debate is clearer for the majority of organizations, particularly small and medium-sized businesses. ITIL 4 already emphasizes governance, therefore COBIT is an unnecessary complication. COBIT is a framework utilized by large established IT organizations. It requires a large number of IT processes and an extensive IT infrastructure to govern. ITIL on the other hand can be a good choice if you are just beginning to build an organization, therefore if you are undecided between COBIT vs ITIL, choose ITIL in the early stages of your ITSM implementation. However after acquiring the necessary skills and experience, you can switch to the enhanced version of ITSM - namely covet. In conclusion, it is up to you to decide how to utilize these magnificent platforms which contain all the pertinent information and key points regarding COBIT and ITIL. COBIT and ITIL are both accountable for ensuring that the company's IT resources enable and enhance all business operations. Both frameworks have a common objective and complement one another in helping organizations achieve this objective. To ensure that businesses implement all processes and strategies effectively, they must provide employees with extensive training in the frameworks and procedures. Implementation and integration are most likely to be successful when conducted by individuals with knowledge and expertise on the subject.

Chapter 26 Incident Management VS Problem Management

Are you confused by the difference between Incident Management and Problem Management? Well, perhaps you have been introduced to the term incident or problem by utilizing some sort of IT Service Management software like Servicenow or Remedy or Hornbill or any of these incident tracking systems that you have and you hear people use the word incident and then problem or then problem, then incident and it seems like, well aren't they talking about the same thing? Actually in the world of ITIL they are not. The difference is going to be what many people might say this sounds like a semantical kind of a thing. You say incident I say problem, I say problem you say incident, but in the world of ITIL as a framework, the incidents do not become problems. It was an incident and now it's a problem. No, instead problems cause incidents. What we find is that anytime you have some sort of product or service that you're delivering whether it's software based or it's maybe like access to something or you build something like a piece of hardware or it could be even service actions that are done behind the scenes that there are always a little bit of the vulnerabilities or errors or issues that are going on and those are what cause the incident. In the world of ITIL they use the word problem instead of an error or a vulnerability. It doesn't mean that we don't use the term error or vulnerability but let's take a look at the definitions. First off an incident according to ITIL is any unplanned interruption which means if there are unplanned interruptions there are planned interruptions things like maintenance or projected service outages - that happens, or any degradation in the quality of an IT Service or any of the IT Service components. For example an incident is something like you try to log into maybe your Sharepoint site or into some sort of service portal and you put in the URL and click on a link and it comes up and it says 404 page not found or unable to connect to the server or some error message and you're like, well great that's where all my stuff is and I need to get to it. That is an interruption and that's an unplanned interruption. You were planning on getting some work done and it didn't happen. Whereas the degradation of quality is you click on the link, you type it in and it loads slowly. Finally you type in your username your password you hit it and it spins and it spins and it times out. There's a degradation in quality. It's not fast or the performance is not what it's supposed to be or maybe there's too many people are logged in but yet there should be plenty of room for people to log into this thing. It doesn't matter, that's a degradation in quality or unplanned interruptions and that's an incident. Then we see problem. Problem is any potential or actual cause of an incident which could be one incident or it could be more incidents it could be more of a cascading effect and this is where those vulnerabilities and errors come in. Incidents are like fires and Problem Management is like arson investigation. Why did the fire start? It could been faulty wiring in your house and triggered a fire, or you're cooking something and someone wasn't paying attention and the grease splattered out and then it started a fire. Why did the fire start? The Incident Management is all about putting out the fire and those can be small fires like type fives up to ones, then you have major incidents which could be a little bit more bigger fire so you would probably spend do something a little bit different for that, whereas Problem Management is why do these things keep happening? This can be both proactive where you take maybe some incident records and look for trends that you notice like every Thursday right around three to five o'clock, we get a lot of people saying that the quality of the data links system is down. Why is that? Thursday is maybe when a lot of people are running some reports, well, then you can find that problem that cause and come up with a resolution so that way you're not having those incidents occur. Or it could be something where you have a major incident or you have something like a security breach or something that's really major and we would say that we definitely need to do Problem Management. Problem Management uses all kinds of different analysis and you create what are known as known errors sometimes where you know about it but you don't have a full resolution you can put in place so you come up with what they call workarounds. You come up with something that's not a full solution but it's more of a mitigating solution where you at least keep it from going to heck in a handbasket real quick. That is going to be where you take Problem Management. Problem Management utilizes things like Kepner and Trigo, the five whys and you can also use technical observation posts where you just literally watch the machine and when it happens you're can see why that happened. These are all techniques that you find the reason and the cause of the incidents. Where incidents you analyze well why is it down, why is it not working and that's where you use the incident analysis you follow your ticketing system you track it you provide good quality updates. So that's the difference between Incident Management, putting out fires and Problem Management which is much more like an arson investigation why did the fire start and why did that incident or these set of incidents start.

Chapter 27 Continual Improvement Model

Your boss is always asking you that you got to make things better and you got to continually improve. What does that mean? Well one of the biggest tenants of the IT Infrastructure Library or ITIL as we call it is continual improvement we're always looking for ways to improve and that's why when your boss or your manager or any of your leadership in your organization is saying we need to make things better and we need to make sure that we're doing these improvement initiatives and we need to do all that kind of stuff and you're like okay, but how to do it well and how to do it efficiently and effectively, which is a big part of ITIL. What we're going to do is we're going to take a look at something that ITIL gives to all of us called the Continual Improvement model or the CI model is what they call it. The continual improvement model is a series of questions and one statement, used to be called the CSI approach or Continual Service Improvement approach and it was only six questions. But as you're going to see they got to the part where you basically says how do we get there and then did we get there and everyone was like well wait a minute we got to do something at some point? So in ITIL 4 they added the statement we actually take action we actually do the work. So let's walk through each one of these steps in the CI model and we are going to use an example. Let's say we have my producer and director who has now been promoted to Service Desk Manager and it they have their customer support and they have their Service Desk where people can call in and if something's going on they need some help. As part of what we see in the Continual Improvement model is ITIL says anytime you do an improvement initiative, anytime you start any of this type of stuff you start with the vision.

That makes it fairly simple. You think well okay I have a vision of what this improvement initiative is supposed to do. But ITIL says you are pretty much hurting yourself unless that improvement initiative vision matches the vision of your business or your organization. The first thing that we see here is what is the vision. The vision is going to be the business vision the mission the goals and objectives. Let's say that part of your vision statement or mission statement says something about we want to have our company should be number one in customer satisfaction of all the companies in the world globally. That's a pretty big vision so how do I tie something like that to an improvement initiative. Well you know what, if I do something in my improvement initiative that matches having high customer satisfaction, the Service Desk is one of the first places you go to take a look at that. FCR or First Contact Resolution and what that means is what it sounds like through the first person you chat with the first person you call or email helps you with your solution that is typically going to raise your customer satisfaction rating. My vision for this initiative is to improve the FCR score for our Service Desk. Great - that's the vision and that's the improvement initiative that you want to do. Well the next thing is anytime you have a journey you got to start somewhere. So the next question is where are we now? This is where you get your current state and this is where you get your baseline of where you're at right now and that way that helps where you can go on that journey. In this case either one of two things will probably happen. Either already measuring on your FCR score at the Service Desk or start to create a baseline and get some data that we can measure against where are we currently at. Whether you already had the information or actually did some measurements, you find out that is at a 68% first time contact or first contact resolution which is actually a pretty good setting. But you want to get better because that will then improve the customer satisfaction of the company. Next step of course is where do you want to be? This is where you set the target or the end game and where you want to be at the end of this improvement initiative and one thing that ITIL says is you should use SMART targets. SMART is an acronym that stands for Specific, Measurable, Achievable or Attainable, Relevant and Time-bound. You need to set a target and doing a little gap analysis and maybe some benchmarking against other Service Desks in the industry and you know what their scores are, you say, I am going to set a target of having a 72% FCR score over the next 90 days. Is that specific? Absolutely. Is that measurable? Of course it's measurable. If you can measure FCR before, you can still measure FCR. Then is it achievable or attainable? That's why if you have done other improvement initiatives similar to this you might have a good idea or you do a little gap analysis or benchmarking and figure out if that's something that you can hit. Is it relevant? Yes it ties into the vision of the organization and the initiative. Is it time bound? Yes, 90 days, so there you go. A lot of times if you're going to be doing these type of improvement initiatives, they're going to be more than just these one or two things, but for our illustrative purposes that's why we're just sticking with this. We already know the vision, we know where we are right now, we know where we want to be so we need to know how do we get there and this is where you put your plan into place. Great thing about the CI model is it's utilized in Agile environments as well as your traditional Waterfall project Management so it doesn't matter which mode or methodology you use, Agile or Waterfall, this model works. You might do a few more iterations in Agile or make it a little bit more repeatable, but for the most part you're going to be following the same thing. You need to define the improvement plan and this is where you sit down with two of the top people on Service Desk and say something like how are we going to make this work? We need to really clean up that knowledge base and if that's a great idea let's make that a part of our plan. Maybe we can bring in our tier 2 and tier 3 folks and double jack in with our first line responders at the Service Desk and they can learn some things from them - just do an hour a week and that way it's not taking their whole week and not taking too much time but if it's one hour a week for each one of those people, we all get to learn a little bit more. Awesome stuff - we have the plan. This is why I said the old CSI approach just immediately went with, did we get there? Well, no. We got to take action! We have to execute on the plan. You are executing on the plan, and once you do that and getting measurements and metrics, at the end though 90 days goes by and guess what? You got to ask the question; did we get there? At this point is where we look at the numbers and say wow - 72.3%! Congratulations! You did it. You hit the target and so you take a look and evaluate the metrics and the KPIs of that improvement initiative. Typically you say what do those numbers look like and is there any other data that I can gather and then kick it into the final step - the seventh step which is how do we keep the momentum going? Because one thing about this term is that it's continual. You don't just do one and done for the next decade and we don't have to do anything else. No, you say it's awesome and that was great so let's take what we've learned and let's improve upon it. That's a part of utilizing the continual improvement CI model to the next time your boss says, let's get better at what we do or when are we going to start improving on things, the CI model is really what you need to use.

Chapter 28 Benefits of Having an ITIL Certification

Is getting certified in the ITIL 4 framework something worth looking into? I mean let's get past the whole Certifications useful debate and assume that they do have worth as companies today are asking are you certified? I'll admit up front that I'm a bit biased towards Certifications as long as they are used correctly. Nothing beats overall experience and work ethic when it comes to working in the industry but Certification does have its usage. I'm an ITIL 4 Managing Professional and ITIL 4 Strategic Leader so I've seen all the certs in this framework up close and personal and I can tell you without any doubt that learning these concepts are useful for you in your day-to-day job. IT Service Managers need good business analysis skills and awareness of their business priorities they need to apply logical thinking and make both day to day and longer term strategic plans to make sure that the business solution aligns with the organization and what the user needs and you also need strong customer service, negotiation, stakeholder and relationship Management capabilities to make sure that supplier and customer needs are met by the service. IT Service Managers and employees need to be good communicators, able to work well with people as well as having a strong motivational and organizational skill set, plus the ability to multitask and that's where ITIL 4 Certification comes in. Think of it as learning the common language of IT Service Management. The practices, the service value system, the guiding principles and all that's included in the ITIL 4 framework - it all works together, and when everyone from the Operations side up to seeing your leadership understand the principles, it really helps align your IT department to the needs of the business. For example consider Spotify. Spotify is the largest global music streaming subscription service out there and it's building this two-sided music marketplace for users and artists and there's a lot going on behind the scenes. You've got data, analytics, software and for artists Spotify provides a platform from which they can then reach out and interact with their fans as well as all the analytics which provides a better and more thorough understanding of what their fan base is, so again, a lot going on. Back in 2017 the organizational growth at Spotify was massive. Teams that were used to working side by side in a smaller environment, now found themselves scattered all around the world and the pending introduction on the stock exchange here in the States it introduced new compliance requirements, so here you go. The organization is experiencing growth pains they need these company-wide policies and common ways of working and that is all increasing. So when the consulting firm that Spotify hired began its assignment to help ITIL as a framework, was relatively unknown within the Spotify organization. In fact some of the staff members felt that using frameworks that's just going to slow us down. However by taking a closer look it proved that very few of the staff members making these remarks had tried ITIL. They had no firsthand experience so the ITIL framework served to guide the work being carried out and implicit references were made to several of the ITIL processes and practices throughout their assignment, including Change Management or now called Change Enablement, demand Management, Incident Management and request fulfilment. Another friend of mine was working for Disney Corporation and at one point the Disney Parks IT Group had all of their it employees get ITIL certified and Managers were tasked to get the ITIL expert Certification. The reason? They were making major changes in how guests access their rooms, paid for food and souvenirs, how do you get in line for rides with the fast pass. They wanted to make sure everyone in IT was on the same page. So getting ITIL 4 certified is definitely a plus when applying for a new job, maybe changing careers, maybe even going for a promotion.

Chapter 29 How to Prepare for ITIL 4 Foundation Exam Online

Since 2021, the ITIL 4 Foundations exam is delivered exclusively online so in this chapter we will walk through some of the common questions that we have. Some basic questions are things like what are the basics of the exam? Whether you're doing this in person or online that has not changed, so the basics are that you have 40 multiple choice questions of varying level of difficulty and you have 60 minutes to complete those 40 questions. They are all worth the same amount of points and you don't get any points attracted by answering the incorrect answer so definitely answer all 40 questions and each question has one answer. It'll either be A or B or C or D. Preparing for the online exam - some things to be aware of, you do want to download software from People Cert, it is called Exam Shield and basically what the software does is that it prevents you from opening up other tabs online and Googling answers. You'll want to download that onto your computer or your laptop and test it out prior to taking the exam. You'll want to test out your microphone, and your sound and too and test out your video too because there will actually be a live proctor watching you during the exam. Once you start the exam though you will forget that they are there, so nothing to worry about in terms of the proctor. You do want to test it without earphones or earbuds. They need to be able to hear you and you aren't able to have earphones in or music playing so just be aware of that. We've had some students where they will test it with earphones in and then the proctor will ask them to take them out and there have been some technical difficulties, so just avoid anything like that. Other things to be aware of, you want to also prepare your room. A lot of us are working from home and at a minimum need to have a clean desk. They will actually ask you to turn your video camera around because they want to see the room and your room can have clutter but you cannot have a desk that has clutter on it. You can't have any notes and in fact this is a closed book exam so no books and no notes. You can have blank paper and a pen or pencil. You'll want to show that to your proctor and you'll want to show them both sides of the paper and then at the end of the exam they'll want you to rip that up and get rid of it just to maintain the integrity of the examination. Do have extra paper with you, do make sure you have a clean desk and you want to be in a quiet space. If you've got a room with a door, they're want to see that make sure that the door is closed that no one's feeding you answers and you don't have any notes with answers around the room. If you have a second monitor, they're going to ask you to cover that with a blanket. As far as what does the user interface look like, it is pretty straightforward. You'll see one question at a time, so once you click start exam a question will pop up and you have the ability to answer it or you can mark it and save it for later. It's a pretty intuitive user interface so you can jump in between questions. I would recommend that if any particular question is giving you problems, just skip that and come back to it later. There will be plenty of time on the exam to go back and review your answers. But will you see your score at the end? Well, you will get a general score. It'll say you got 37 out of 40 correct and it'll tell you in general areas kind of where you're stronger or weaker so it'll say like general concepts, you're this percent, or Service Management practices you got this percent correct. But it won't tell you each answer if was correct or not. To maintain the integrity of the examination, you really don't get a ton of information but it will tell you a little bit around where you're strong and where you're weak on the exam and you will get a final exam score. You will know that immediately as soon as you click submit and once you pass the exam you'll have access to your online certificate. But are there any other exam test taking tips? Well, I would say you should take your time on this exam. Take the full hour if you need it. You do want to get

26 out of the 40 questions correct, so don't leave any easy ones on the table and make sure that you're going back to the ones that you're marking and with every question make sure that you read the full question you read all four of the answers fully and make sure that you're answering to what they're asking. You've probably taken practice exam questions or if you haven't yet you will, leading up to the exam but don't make the assumption that what you see on the exam is exactly what you may have seen on a practice exam question because words matter and if they change one word that could change the whole intent of the question. So just be careful and slow down and take your time, you've got this! But what do you need to have with you for the exam itself? Well, you also want to have your ID with you because before they start the exam, they want to actually confirm that it's you taking the exam and not your best friend that's willing to help you by taking the exam for you which would be an awesome friend. They want to confirm that it's actually you so you'll have to hold up your ID and show them that it is in fact the same person that's on the ID that has registered for the exam that's actually taking the exam. Other things that they will ask you to move out of your way when you take the exam is if you have your cell phone or a smart watch, you'll need to show them that you're putting it out of arm's reach because it is a closed book exam they also don't want you texting anyone for the answers or casually looking at your smartphone or smartwatch and getting answers that way. So just be aware that they'll make you put all those things away at the start of the exam.

The first question is how does the services practice contribute to the engaged service value chain activity.

How does the Service Desk Practice contribute to the *Engage* Service Value Chain activity?

A. By coordinating all activities during the rollout of new applications
B. By ensuring that all stakeholders have been engaged in the definition of SLAs
C. By acting as the main channel for operational engagement with users
D. By providing first level support for customers

The right answer in this case is C. By coordinating all the activities during the rollout of new applications in A is not true because for that we have release Management and deployment Management to work in conjunction to achieve this goal. B says by ensuring that all stakeholders have been engaged in the definition of SLAs. Certainly an interesting option but surely not the services practice they might be engaged in the definition of SLAs but it's not their task to coordinate all the activities. That is the responsibility of service level Management. By acting as the main channel for operational engagement with users - that is the correct answer because it's all about engaging with the users at the Service Desk. They call the Service Desk, and they email them and they chat and they reach the Service Desk in any other way and the main responsibility of the Service Desk is to answer those operational activities and questions and inquiries the users and customers might have. Then D says by providing first level support for customers which is kind of true but C is even better because it has a broader spectrum and it's a bigger range than just simply providing first level support for the customers.

Question number two who are the main parties involved in the definition of SLAs or service level agreements?

Who are the main parties involved in the definition of SLAs?

A.Service Provider and Customer
B.Customer and Vendor
C.Vendor and Service Provider
D.IT and Business

The correct answer to this question is A because the SLAs are defined between service provider and customer. They tell the service provider what levels of service would make our customers satisfied and what we should deliver to make them happy. B says customer and vendor but honestly most of the times we as a service provider don't care about all the other vendors our customers might have, except if we are involved in service integration Management. Then we have answer C which says vendor and service provider and that is a special contract also defined in ITIL but it's called underpinning contract or UC. Then we have IT and business as answer option D which is we can call internal parties of the same service provider organization and if they have an agreement between each other that would be called an OLA or operational level agreement.

Question 3 why should you utilize a CMDB or Configuration Management Database within your organization?

Why should you utilize a CMDB within your organization?

A. To get an overview of all your CIs and understand their relationships
B. Because there is a regulatory requirement for it
C. To track all hardware related Incidents
D. To ensure that only approved versions are used when installing software

The correct answer is A in this case. It says to get an overview of all your CI's or configuration items and understand their relationships. That is the main goal of the configuration Management practice and with it of the Configuration Management Database. You want to know what you have in your organization; all the servers and applications that run on it, the services which you have and also the individual infrastructure elements like routers, switches, firewalls, printers, wireless access points and so one and you want to understand how those components work together. B says because there is a regulatory requirement for it. It might be the case but it's certainly not the main goal. C says to track all hardware related Incidents. Well it is an advantage to be able to do this by having a CMDB in place but it's not the main goal. D says to ensure that only approved versions are used when installing software and that is ensured by a special part of the CMDB which is called DML or definitive media library which holds all the approved versions of software applications which then can be pushed to the individual workstations and servers when needed.

Question 4; The Problem Management practice is meant to... to what exactly?

The Problem Management practice is meant to...?

A. Reduce the number of Problems
B. Resolve Incidents that cannot be solved by the Service Desk
C. Identify and solve the unknown cause of one or more Incidents
D. Enable the expert teams to troubleshoot complex issues

The correct answer for this is C. It says identify and solve the unknown cause of one or more Incidents. That is it by definition. The problem by definition is the unknown cause of one or more Incidents and the Problem Management practice is meant to identify those and solve those problems to make sure they never happen again. The goal is also to reduce the number of recurring Incidents but then if you look at A reduce the number of problems, that's not a goal. It might sound like it but it's not. It's goal is to identify root causes and to make sure that the Incidents resulting out of these problems do not reoccur. B says resolve Incidents that cannot be solved by the Service Desk. Certainly not true again because that is still the Incident Management practice. It's just other support teams like second level teams or expert teams who are supposed to do exactly this. Then we have D which says enable expert teams to troubleshoot complex issues. Again not the case. We don't open a problem ticket just because an Incident ticket gets too complex. We open problem tickets if we don't know what is causing these Incident tickets.

Question number five; which guiding principle emphasizes the need to understand the flow of work, identify bottlenecks and remove waste?

Which guiding principle emphasizes the need to understand the flow of work, identify bottlenecks and remove waste?

A. Progress Iteratively With Feedback
B. Start Where You Are
C. Keep It Simple And Practical
D. Collaborate And Promote Visibility

The right answer is D. D says collaborate and promote visibility and that guiding principle certainly has a goal to ensure that whatever blocks our work is made visible. Then we have transparency and that we collaborate with other teams and stakeholders to remove those bottlenecks which will enable us to speed up the floor work and get results done faster. A says progress iteratively with feedback which is one of my favorite guiding principles, nonetheless it's not the right one for this question because it's more about the baby steps and the continual feedback from our stakeholders. B; start where you are is all about utilizing what is already in place instead of building or buying everything from zero so we can make sure that we recycle stuff that can still be used. C says keep it simple and practical which speaks for itself. Sure we shouldn't overdo stuff we don't need the gold plating but we barely need what the customer requires. We shouldn't over achieve nor underachieve but the correct answer for this question is the collaborate and promote visibility.

Question number six; the percentage of successful versus failed changes is an example of what?

The percentage of successful versus failed Changes is an example of what?

A. A Practice Success Factor
B. A Key Performance Indicator
C. A Performance Goal
D. A Critical Success Factor

The right answer in this case is B. It is a Key Performance Indicator or KPI. It's a typical metric which helps us to measure how well our practices are working. The first one says a practice success factor which is more like an overarching goal that our practice needs to achieve, but it's not an individual metric. A performance goal is something completely different and not even defined in ITIL like that and a critical success factor is the old name of practice success factors. So the correct answer here is a KPI.

Question 7 says reusing resources if possible is a recommendation of which guiding principle?

Reusing resources if possible is a recommendation of which Guiding Principle?

A.Start Where You Are
B.Focus on Value
C.Keep It Simple And Practical
D.Optimize And Automate

Well, the correct answer for this question is A. It says start where you are. Start where you are is all about making sure that whatever we have already in place is somehow utilized again if possible. Just because we are installing a new application, it doesn't mean we need to buy everything. Maybe we already have some servers available or maybe we have some human resources available which will help us install that application on those servers and configure those. So we don't need to start from zero - that's the message of this guiding principle. Focus on value says that we should understand our stakeholders and what is important to our stakeholders. Keep it simple and practical says we shouldn't overachieve and we shouldn't overdo but simply achieve what is needed by our customers and stakeholders. D says optimize and automate and the main message here is that we should automate whatever is possible in an economical manner to maximize the value of human work. Whatever can be automated should be automated because then we can invest our own time into more value-focused activities.

Question 8 says what is the perceived benefit, usefulness, and importance of something?

What is the perceived benefit, usefulness, and importance of something?

A. A Service
B. A Practice
C. Utility
D. Value

The correct answer for this question is D - it is value. Services are the means of enabling value co-creation with our customers. A practice is a configuration of resources that is somehow transforming input into output and utility is part of the value. It is telling us how useful a service is but it's not the only part, and value is the perceived benefits. I like to highlight the fact that it says perceived benefits because you can have the best utility and you can have the best warranty, which is another part of what value is, but it's also about the perception of your customers. If they have a bad feeling or if they think badly or if they have bad experiences with your services besides that, then you will have a hard time.

Question 9 says moving configurations from one environment to the next is done by which practice?

Moving configurations from one environment to the next is done by which Practice?

A. Release Management
B. Deployment Management
C. Configuration Management
D. Asset Management

The correct answer for this question is B or deployment Management because answer A; release Management is responsible for the coordination of the activities that are needed to make services available for customers and users. This may include also the movement of configuration from one environment to the next but it's only the coordination that is done and not the doing itself because that is deployment Management. Configuration Management ensures that we have a CMDB in place that we understand, what configuration items we have and how they connect to each other. And then we have asset Management which considers the financial impact of our IT assets.

Question 10 says how does the Service Request practice contribute to the obtain build service value chain activity?

> **How does the Service Request Practice contribute to the *Obtain/Build* Service Value Chain activity?**
>
> A. Delivery of support via the Service Desk
> B. Management of all pre-defined Standard Changes
> C. Acquisition of pre-approved service components may be fulfilled through service requests
> D. Correct categorization of Service Request Tickets

The right answer for this question is C. A says delivery of support via the service test practice and this is not true because that would be the service test practice and not the Service Request practice. B says Management of all predefined standard changes. Well, the Service Request practice kind of does that but it doesn't do it in the obtain and build service value chain activity, rather in the deliver and support. Then we have D which says correct categorization of Service Request tickets. Again it's done this in the deliver and support service value chain activity, so the correct one here is C, the acquisition of pre-approved service components may be fulfilled through Service Requests. This means that whenever we need to buy something and to build and configure our service or our products and for this we need some kind of predefined standard items - let's say like laptops or phones - then we could open Service Requests for this and get them done by the Service Request practice instead of opening changes which need to go through the usual change approval procedure. Therefore the correct answer here is C.

Question 11 says what is the difference between an Incident and a Service Request?

What is the difference between an Incident and a Service Request?

A. Incidents are handled by expert teams, while Service Request are solved at the Service Desk
B. Incidents are requests for solutions while Service Requests are requests for information or other standard services
C. Incidents are handled for free, while Service Requests are paid for
D. Incidents must be categorized, while Service Requests mustn't

The correct answer for this question is B. It says Incidents are requests for solutions while Service Requests are requests for Information or other standard services. Well, Incidents are things that have been working before but are not working right now, so we need to make sure that we put back the operation into the usual way of working as soon as possible and that is what Incidents are for; providing solutions. Service Requests there are requests for everything else like Information when a user calls a Service Desk and asks how something can be done or where they can find some specific Information or maybe they need access to some resources - that's all Service Requests. A says Incidents are handled by expert teams while Service Requests are solved at the Service Desk and that's not exactly true. It's true but it's not only the case. Incidents are also handled by the Service Desk and by second or third level teams, by developers, by application support or infrastructure support as well as Service Requests. There might be cases where

Service Requests are also handled not at the Service Desk but at other support teams. C says Incidents are handled for free while Service Requests are paid for. While this might be the case in some companies as you never know about the operational model of different service providers, but it's not part of the ITIL 4 Foundation course to say that this is the way how it needs to be done. D says Incidents must be categorized by Service Requests mustn't. It's not the case. Both should be categorized for better reporting and evaluation afterwards.

Question number 12; the following is an example of what? A company has agreed with its customers that the availability of a cloud application must be above 99.4%.

The following is an example of what?

A company has agreed with its customer that the availability of a cloud application must be above 99.4%.

A.Operational Level Agreement (OLA)
B.Contract
C.Performance Goal
D.Service Level Agreement (SLA)

The correct answer for this one is D - it's a service level agreement because it says a company has agreed with its customer and service level agreements are contracts or agreements between service providers and their customers. An operational level agreement would be true if it would be an agreement between different parts of the same organization and while B, which says a contract might be true, an SLA is not always to be seen as a binding contract. Usually if you have an external customer who buys your service, it is a contract, but the correct answer here is D because in the first place it's a service level agreement and only in the second place it might be a contract. Then C says it's a performance goal. While it might be true that it is a performance goal, ITIL 4 doesn't talk about performance goal in these capabilities or in these capacities.

Question number 13 says if the... step of the continual improvement model is skipped, we will not be able to understand if an initiative reached its goal. So which step are we talking about?

> **If the _____ step of the Continual Improvement Model is skipped, we will not be able to understand if an initiative reached its goal.**
>
> A. Did we get there?
> B. How do we get there?
> C. Take action
> D. How do we keep the momentum going?

The correct answer for this one is A; did we get there? because it ensures that once we reached a certain stage in our project or initiative, we reflect back on the original plan that we wanted to achieve because earlier in the continual improvement model, there was a question which says where do we want to be and there we defined measurable targets, which will lead us to our overall goal in achieving our strategy and our vision and in a step did we get there, we compare those measurable goals with the actual results to see if we reach these and if we are in the right way. B says how do we get there that's a little bit earlier. It thinks about how we would like to achieve these goals, like which Project Management methodology would like to choose or how do we want to achieve what we plan for. C says take action. Kind of speaks for itself so we would act upon the plan of our initiative or of our project that we want to implement. And D says how do we keep the momentum going which is all about once we implemented this new way of working - this new initiative or this new whatever we were doing, then we need to make sure that people keep it working so that they don't fall back to the old ways of working before. We need to ensure a quality control that that people will not just go back to how it was before because it's often much easier than to work in a new way or once something new has been implemented to make that work better.

Question 14 says which of the following is NOT a part of the service value system?

Which of the following is NOT a part of the Service Value System?

A. Management
B. Governance
C. The Practices
D. Continual Improvement

The correct answer is A because it's Management. In the service value system we have the guiding principles, we have governance, the practices, the continual improvement and the center piece is the service value chain. Input is always opportunity and demand and the output is always value. While we do need Management, we have not defined it as a major part or as a main part of the service value system because the Management of our services is the whole thing that we are doing anyway. It's a whole Service Management part and then the governance part also contains some Management, ensuring that we reach our KPIs and then we reach our defined goals. But it's not a separate part of the service value system.

Question number 15 says how does the configuration Management practice support the deliver and support service value chain activity?

> ## How does the Configuration Management practice support the *Deliver and Support* Service Value Chain activity?
>
> A. It delivers essential information to planning activities related to the Service Configurations of the organization
> B. It provides financial information about the usage of services and CIs
> C. For the effective solution of Incidents and Problems, information about CIs is essential
> D. Without a CMDB no ticketing system is able to function

The correct answer is C. It says for the effective solution of incidence and problems Information about CI's or configuration items is essential and that is so true. Delivery and support is all about the operational part of our services, making sure that it runs as needed so it's all about handling Incidents and it's all about the Service Desk and it's about the problems that we need to handle. And if we want to make sure that we handle them most effectively, we should understand the relationship about our configuration items. How they connect to each other, which server relates to which other services and which applications are running on which computer and which laptop is on whose user's name and so on, and it's all part of the configuration Management practice and within it, the Configuration Management Database. A says it delivers essential Information to planning activities related to the service configuration of the organization which it really does, but that one doesn't relate to deliver and support service value chain activity, but to the plan service value chain activity. B says it provides financial Information about the usage of services and configuration items. Not true because that is asset Management. D says without the CMDB or Configuration Management Database no ticketing system is able to function. Not correct! They are able to function, though I must admit it's much better if you have a nice CMDB within your organization because it allows for much better tracking and reporting if you have the possibility to connect your tickets like Incidents or problems or changes with configuration items that you have in your system. So you have let's say a clear link which user open which ticket or which laptop has which ticket connected to it or which server has the most problem tickets connected to it because these kinds of trends can be identified later on and then permanent solutions can be found.

Question 16 says; You are the newly appointed service Manager in a large international corporation. Which guiding principle will help you understand what is already in place in the IT department that could be utilized for your new ideas?

You are the newly appointed Service Manager in a large international corporation. Which Guiding Principle will help you understand what is already in place in the IT department that could be utilized for your new ideas?

A. Focus on value
B. Start where you are
C. Progress iteratively with feedback
D. Keep it simple and practical

The correct answer for this is B; start where you are because that is all about measurement. It's all about getting a picture of the current situation of your organization, your people, your infrastructure or the resources that are available before you jump into any new initiative or before you can start building your new ideas. You need to have a picture of what you have right now because that can be reused and it can be recycled instead of buying new stuff all the time or building things from scratch. You might want to have a look around to see what can be reused because otherwise if you build everything from scratch or buy everything new it's just a waste of resources. Try to use what you already have in place. Focus on value is certainly a good guiding principle as well because it helps you understand what your customers need and want, but it's not about understanding what you currently have in place. C says progress iteratively with feedback which would be utilized once you have an idea what your customers want and you understand what you already have because then you can start building things that you don't have or buying things - procuring things that you don't have and that should be done in an Agile way in an iterative manner, while you get a lot of feedback from your customers which will keep you on track all the time, which reassures you that you are doing the right thing. D says keep it simple and practical which is certainly a nice guiding principle and I would certainly suggest to keep this in mind all the time because we shouldn't over achieve because it's just unnecessarily expensive. We should try to focus on what our customers want - focus on value and then try to achieve exactly that because nobody's going to pay us for overachieving stuff.

Question 17 says The uncertainty of an outcome is called?

The uncertainty of an outcome is called what?

A.An opportunity
B.A hazard
C.A change
D.A Risk

The correct answer for this question id D which says it's a risk. A - an opportunity is a risk as well but it's a positive risk. B says a hazard which is also risk just a negative kind. C says a change which is the modification or addition of anything related to our configuration items, which can have an effect on our service delivery and D or risk is by definition the uncertainty of an outcome. You just simply don't know what's going to happen. It might be good, it might be bad but it's a risk and it needs to be managed it needs to be evaluated and we as a service provider organization need to understand if we want to take that risk, if it's worth it or if it's not worth it and we want to mediate it somehow or try to find a solution for it.

Question number 18 say what are the two triggers of the service value system or SVS?

What are the two triggers of the Service Value System (SVS)?

A. Services and Value
B. Chances and Demand
C. Demand and Opportunities
D. Requirements and Opportunities

The right answer for this question is C. Demand and opportunities are the input because it might come from our customers and that they tell us they need something, that would be a new demand but it might also be the case that we do some market research or we just read about some cool new Technology or somebody in the company has ideas about a possibility that might provide value to our customers, so these are opportunities. A says services and value. Well no because services are the means of enabling value co-creation to our customers and value is the output of the service value system. Chances are in demand it's 50% true but it's not called chances - it's called opportunities and D says requirements and opportunities - again 50% true because it's not called requirements - it's called demand and opportunities. So the correct answer is C; demand and opportunities.

Question 19 says how does the Information security Management practice support the design and transition service value chain activity?

The correct answer here is C. It says by ensuring that effective security controls are designed and transitioned into live environments. That is exactly what design and transition is about. It's about making sure that whatever we are, whatever we identified as valuable to the customer we need to give it a little bit more thought and you do a little bit deeper planning in the design phases and then we need to make sure that it is transitioned from development environments to test to prod effectively where it can then be supported by delivery and support. A says by handling all security related Incidents - not true because that is the Incident Management practice. B says by enabling the CISO or Chief Information Security Officer to prevent penetration attacks and while good designs might prevent penetration attacks, it's not only about the Chief Information Security Officer because he might also have or she might also have people in their team or it might also be the Service Desk or it might be any employee who can prevent security attacks. D says by defining the priority of security related issues and that's again like A the Incident Management practice.

Question 20 say you have been named IT Service Desk Lead in your organization but users complain that the quality is strongly varying depending on which agent they talk to. What should you do?

You have been named IT Service Desk Lead in your organization. Users complain that the quality is strongly varying depending on which Agent they talk to. What should you do?

A. Introduce text scripts to be used by Agents, defining how to handle different situations in a standard way
B. Ask the user for the names of the Agents so you can talk to them
C. Escalate this situation immediately to your superior
D. Generate reports on the amount of tickets handled by each Agent and analyse them for issues in the documentation

The correct answer for this one is A. What should we do? Well let's introduce text scripts to be used by our agents, defining how to handle different situations in a standard way. Predefined text elements they can use for the handling of different issues or maybe for the handling of different customers or difficult customers because that would allow us to create a standard quality because all of our agents would be communicating with the same quality. B says ask the user for the names of the agents so you can talk to them. While it might certainly be a good thing to talk to your people, nevertheless it's not a quality insurance and on the other side I'm not sure that all the users would remember all the names of the agents they ever talked to. C says escalate the situation immediately to your superior. Well that would not be a very nice thing to do. Maybe first you should talk to your people or first you should understand the situation a little bit better before you escalate directly to your Manager. Then D says generate reports on the amount of tickets handled by each agent and analyze them for issues in the documentation. While issues in the documentation might lead to quality problems, it will not help you to understand how the agent talks to the customer on the phone. There might be huge differences in written documentation and spoken communication, so it's much better to introduce text scripts as said in answer A.

Our 21st question is what is the goal of the monitoring and event Management practice?

> ## What is the goal of the Monitoring and Event Management practice?
>
> A. To protect the information that an organization needs for business
> B. To restore normal service operation as soon as possible
> C. To observe services and components, and to record any changes in their state
> D. To provide accurate and reliable information about CIs when needed

The correct answer for this question is C. It says; to observe services and components and to record any changes in their state. This is the purpose statement of the monitoring and event Management practices. We want to make sure that we can monitor what is happening in our infrastructure and our services and we can make sense of those things. When something is happening we need to categorize those events and we need to make sure that we understand what to do with those. It could be Informational type of events or it could be warning events but it could also be exceptions like Incidents that something broke and we need to fix it. A is to protect the Information that an organization needs for business. That would be the Information security Management practice. Then we have B to restore normal service operation as soon as possible which would be the Incident Management practice and D to provide accurate and reliable Information about CIs when needed and that would be the configuration Management practice.

Question number 22; you have been tasked with the setup of an internal Service Desk in the small company you work for. Ensuring that the right tools and applications will be used by the team is a consideration of which Service Management dimension?

You have been tasked with the setup of an internal Service Desk in the small company you work for. Ensuring that the right tools and applications will be used by the team is a consideration of which Service Management Dimension?

A. Information and Technology
B. Partners and Suppliers
C. Organization and People
D. Value Streams and Processes

The correct answer for this question is A. It's Information and Technology because that is what it is about exactly this. It's about understanding what technological stuff and what tools and what Information we need to be able to run or make our new initiative work. If we want to build up a new services, we need to think about all the tools, also the computers and also the Information like building up a knowledge base and which tool to use for building up a knowledge base, how to handle incoming calls, what type of phones we want to have, which type of video or an audio conferencing software do we want to use and so on. B says partners and suppliers would be true if we are thinking about which partners could supply us with these things. What the vendor companies are there on the market which best fit our profile and our needs. C says organization and people would consider the knowledge and the human resources that would be necessary to run this new Service Desk. How many people do we want to hire, what kind of skills do they need, what languages do they need to speak and so on. Answer D; Value streams and processes would consider how the work would be organized on the Service Desk, what would be the things that the Service Desk should do like password resets or maybe it's just a catch and dispatch Service Desk and it just takes the tickets and sends it to the next support levels, so the correct answer for this one is A; Information and Technology.

Question 23 says how does the Service Desk practice support the deliver and support service value chain activity?

How does the Service Desk practice support the *Deliver and Support* Service Value Chain activity?

A. By ensuring the correct categorization of all Change Requests
B. By enabling the organization to select the right vendors
C. By allowing the Service Desk Agents to handle all access requests
D. By acting as the central coordination point for the handling of Incidents and Service Requests

The correct answer for this one is D. It says the Service Desk acts as a central coordination point for the handling of Incidents and Service Requests and so it is. It should be the single point of contact or at least a single point of entry for all types of user requests that are coming into the IT organization, mainly talking about Incidents and Service Requests but not necessarily only. It could also handle changes or problem tickets. It surely depends on how you set up your Service Desk, but by default it's about Incident and Service Request handling and acting as a main entry point. A is not true because there will be any support team who is involved in the Change Enablement practice. B says by enabling the organization to select the right vendors. Not true because that will be the supplier Management practice. C says by allowing the Service Desk agents to handle all access requests. Still not true. It might be the case but usually not everything is handled by the Service Desk. There might be setups where certain second level teams or certain expert teams in your organization handle access requests as well.

Question 24 says why is customer engagement crucial for the service level Management practice?

Why is customer engagement crucial for the Service Level Management practice?

A. It defines who is allowed to open Incident tickets from the customer organization
B. It ensures that we meet the agreed service levels
C. It captures information on which metrics can be based
D. It defines the workflow of Service Requests

The correct answer for this question would be C. Why? Because it says it captures Information on which metrics can be based and it's so true. We need to engage with our

163

customers to understand what is important for them. We need to find out what is valuable and then when we are setting up our SLAs and our KPIs and our metrics, we can base these metrics on the Information that the customer engagement delivers to us. We talk to the customers, we understand what they want and then we can build meaningful metrics to measure that they get what they need. A says it defines who is allowed to open Incident tickets from the customer organization. Well not true because that's definitely everybody. B says it ensures that we meet the agreed service levels - not sure because that would be the service level Management practice itself and the reporting that is done within the practice and all the people who are involved in the practice like the service level Manager but even the services team leads even the Service Desk agents would be involved in that. And D says it defines a workflow for Service Requests. Not true because that is the Service Request Management practice.

Question number 25 says why is it important to categorize Incident tickets?

Why is it important to categorize Incident tickets?

A. Because it is a requirement coming from most of the customers and it is a measure of quality

B. It gives us the possibility to identify trends, which might trigger the provision of permanent solutions via Problem Management and Change Enablement

C. If it is not done, we do not know, which customer opens the most tickets

D. Neglecting the categorization might cause financial penalties if the organization gets controlled by external auditor companies

The correct answer for this question would be B. It says it gives us the possibility to identify trends which might trigger the provision of permanent solutions via Problem Management and Change Enablement and that is the correct one because if we can categorize Incidents, we have the possibility to run some meaningful reporting and identify if there are recurring Incidents on the same configuration items or maybe the same applications are down all the time or maybe it's the same services affected and then we can run root cause analysis through Problem Management to find out what is happening and then maybe we need to open a change request to get this solved for good. A says it's a measure of quality. Well it might be a measure of quality and it might be a requirement for most customers but it's still not true. ITIL doesn't talk about that we need to do something because it's a requirement for most customers. C says if it is not done we don't know which customer opens the most tickets. Well that doesn't make any sense because we have the possibility to run reports on the people on the names who opens tickets but in the end it's not even most of the times it's not even a relevant metric that we want to measure. D says neglecting the categorization might cause financial penalties if organizations get controlled by external auditor companies, which might be the case but ITIL doesn't talk about that, so we should do the categorization to have a possibility of identifying trends, so the correct answer is B.

Question 26 says; the handling of user feedbacks compliments and complaints is a responsibility of which practice?

The handling of user feedbacks, compliments and complaints is a responsibility of which practice?

A. Service Desk
B. Service Request Management
C. Incident Management
D. Problem Management

The correct one here is B. It's a tricky one because A says is a Service Desk which is very close to the truth, but it's not only about feedbacks, complaints and the compliments. The Service Desk also handles Incidents and maybe even other types of tickets like changes or problems, so the correct answer is Service Request Management because all types of feedbacks compliments and complaints because they are not Incidents and because they are not changes and not problems and that's why they are handled by the Service Request Management practice. Still the services does it most of the time but not only. It could also be that a certain special team handles all user feedbacks, complements and complaints like a quality team or something like that, so that's why B is the correct answer. Incident Management will be handling all the Incidents and Problem Management all the problems so they are easy to close out.

166

Question 27; how does the Service Request Management practice support the engage service value chain activity?

How does the Service Request Management practice support the *Engage* Service Value Chain activity?

A. By providing regular communication to users to gather requirements, set expectations and to provide updates
B. By handling all user-initiated Service Request and Incidents
C. By communicating Known Errors to the user community
D. By handling the distribution of incoming calls at the Service Desk

The correct answer for this question would be A. A says by providing regular communication to users to gather requirements, set expectations and to provide updates. That is all the engagement that is happening in Service Request Management. If it's the Service Desk who does it or if it's other support teams who do it but it's all about the engagement around Service Requests to understand what the customer needs and also to set expectations to tell them what to expect regarding the resolution times of Service Requests because that's usually more than with Incidents our SLAs allow us, usually more time to get Service Requests done, and also to provide updates because there will be customers who'll be asking like I've ordered a laptop when do I finally receive it and then Service Request Management says yeah it's going to be in two weeks or depending on the vendor or our stock. B says by handling all user-initiated Service Requests and Incidents. That is not true because that would be the Service Desk and it would do it in the deliver and support service value chain activity and not an engage. C says by communicating known errors to the user community. Not true because that would be the Problem Management practice but it would be an engage. D says by handling the distribution of incoming cars at the Service Desk. That wouldn't be a practice. It would be usually a tool like some kind of call center application that would make sure that agents get the cause based on their skills and availability, so the correct answer in this case is A.

Question 28 says which of the following is true for change authorization?

Which of the following is TRUE for Change authorization?

A. Changes should be authorized by one person to speed up the process and to reduce dependencies
B. Normal Changes must be authorized quickly as they require fast actions
C. Each change model and type should have its own Change Authority
D. Standard Changes have a high risk and need to be approved by the management

The correct answer for this question is C which says each change model and type should have its own change authority because a change authority is not a predefined person or anything like that but it needs to be defined based on a type of change. If we have a more significant type of change, it might need to be a separate team like a change advisory board who needs to approve it like the IT Management team or something like that. But if it's a small change it might be even one single person or maybe somebody in the team who can improve it, so that's the concept of decentralized decision making which is promoted in all Agile methodologies and frameworks. A says changes should be authorized by one person to speed up the process and to reduce dependencies. Well we might certainly reduce dependencies but what happens if that person doesn't have the technical knowledge to approve or what if that person is on vacation or maybe that person is sick, the whole process is halted again, so we shouldn't do that. B says normal changes must be authorized quickly as they require fast actions. Not true because there will be emergency changes. D says standard changes have a high risk and need to be approved by the Management. Again not true because standard changes are the exact opposite. They are low cost, low risk pre-approved changes, usually something like Service Requests. Stuff that happens all the time that doesn't need to be approved individually every time somebody opens a standard change, so the correct answer is C.

Question 29 says which is true for problems and known errors?

Which is TRUE for Problems and Known Errors?

A. A Problem is called a Know Error once the root cause has been identified
B. Problems are handled by technical staff, while Known Errors are handled by the Service Desk
C. A Problem is the cause of one or more Known Errors
D. Problems can be closed once they have become Known Errors

The correct answer for this one is A. It says that a problem is called a known error once the root cause has been identified. That is exactly it. The problem by definition is the unknown cause of one or more Incidents and then we start analyzing it because we don't know what's causing it - unknown cause. So we start analyzing what the problem is and then we find something that is causing it. We find a root cause we cannot call a problem anymore because it's not the unknown cause of incidence anymore. It's now the known cause and that's why we call it known error. That's the official term. So once we identify the cause of a problem it's a known error. B says problems are handled by technical stuff while known errors are handled by the Service Desk. Not true because even the services could handle problems and also the second level or technical stuff could also create known errors which are then made available for the Service Desk, which are then made available for communication to the end users. C says a problem is the cause of one or more known errors. Not true at all because a problem is the unknown cause of one or more Incidents. D says problems can be closed once they have become known errors. Not true because it just means that we have identified the root cause which is already a great step but we still need to solve it and we might even need to involve a Change Enablement to get this permanently solved.

Question 30 says the decision about which vendors to engage with is influenced mostly by which of the following?

The decisions about which vendors to engage with is influenced mostly by which of the following?

A. The level of formality in the organization
B. The culture of the service provider organization
C. The contracts the organization has with its own customers
D. The financial strategy of the service provider organization

The correct one here is B. It is about the culture of the service provider organization. We need to think about our vendors as partners with whom we need to engage a lot and we need to select vendors with whom we can work well together. So if we have the possibility to choose because there are vendors with similar offerings, we should always go for the one which fits best into our organizational and into our corporate culture because that would ease the engagement with them a lot. A says the level of formality in the organization which is part of the culture as well somehow but it's not the main reason on which we should base the selection of our vendors, because that's simply not enough. Just because we are very formal doesn't mean that we need to go for a very formal vendor. It's more about the cultural aspect. C says the contracts that the organization has with its own customers. Well it's true at some point but we should make sure that the contracts which we have with our vendors - once we selected them, they should support the SLAs that we have with our own customers. But it's not about the selection at all. It's not about what type of vendor or which vendor we select. It's just about how we define the underpinning contracts with our vendors and that is influenced by the contracts we have with our own customers. D says the financial strategy of the service provider organization. Well it might have an effect on which vendors we select because we might have a strategy to always go for the cheapest one, but that is certainly not a good practice and not even a best practice, so we shouldn't do that.

Question number 31 says by which of the following terms is the functionality of a service or component known in the ITIL framework?

By which of the following terms is the functionality of a service or component known in the ITIL framework?

A. Usability
B. Value
C. Warranty
D. Utility

The correct answer for this question would be D. It is called the utility which means if it is fit for purpose it's a question if it does, what it is supposed to do because every service or component has a practice and if it can fulfill its purpose then it has the right utility. A says usability which is not a term defined in ITIL separately. B says value which is the perceived benefits and usefulness of something and C says warranty which is more about the fitness for usability of a service or component. Utility means if it does what it does and warranty means how well it does what it does so it's mostly about availability, continuity, capacity and security of a service or component.

Question number 32 says how does the Information security Management practice support the deliver and support service value chain activity?

How does the Information Security Management practice support the *Deliver and Support* Service Value Chain activity?

A. By ensuring that effective security policies are in place
B. By efficiently enforcing security policies
C. By including security related considerations into our SLAs
D. By detecting and solving information security related Incidents

The correct answer for this one would be A. It says by ensuring that effective security policies are in place. It is all about having security policies which define what we are supposed to do and how we are supposed to handle and secure the Informational assets of our organization. What kind of passwords to use, how to protect our shared drives and policies for proxy settings for the internet usage or file sharing and so on. B says by efficiently enforcing security policies which is happening in the deliver and support service value chain activity but it would much more be the access Management practice or maybe even the Service Request Management practice. C says by including security related consideration into our SLAs, which is the Information security Management practice, but it would be happening in the design and transition service value chain activity, while the SLAs are defined with our customers and stakeholders. D says by detecting and solving Information security related

Incidents, which is deliver and support but it would be the Incident Management practice.

Question number 33 says continual improvement related decisions should always be based on what?

Continual Improvement related decisions should always be based on ____ .

A. A SWOT (Strengths, Weaknesses, Opportunities, Threats) analysis
B. An evaluated MVP (Minimum Viable Product)
C. Accurately measured and meticulously analyzed data
D. User and Customer feedback

The correct answer for this would be C which says accurately measured and meticulously analyzed data. This is it. We need to make sure that whatever decision we make especially improvement decisions should always be based on accurate data because only that is impartial. If we have valid data on our hands, we can make a clear decision and we can involve the right stakeholders and then the decision will be based on actual data and not just on a gut feeling or on preferences on people because data is impartial. A says SWOT analyzes strength weaknesses opportunities and threats which is also not a very bad option but it's quite a static thing in most organizations. It's not updated frequently so not all of our continual improvement decisions should be based on that. B says an evaluated MVP or minimum viable product which is technically just a small piece of functionality which has been developed and is potentially

175

valuable to our customers, so not all continual improvement decisions should be based on that because it's just a very small fragment of what we are doing of what our capabilities are and what our service solutions might be. D says user and customer feedback which is not a bad option, nevertheless not all of the continual improvement decisions should be based on that because user and customer feedback is not very impartial. It's a lot about gut feelings and about perception of our customers, how they perceive our services, maybe our Service Desk, maybe have specific preferences so it would be a biased decision, so the correct answer for this one would be C.

Question number 34 says continually co-creating value with stakeholders in line with the organization's objectives is a purpose of which of the following?

Continually co-creating value with stakeholders in line with the organization's objectives is a purpose of which of the following?

A. The Service Value System
B. The Service Value Chain
C. Service Management
D. The Seven Guiding Principles

The correct answer for this one would be A. It is the service value system which is about continuous co-creation of value with our organization's customers and stakeholders, because they need to tell what they need and we're going to make sure that we can deliver just that. The service value chain transforms demand into value in the end but it's a deeper level. It's not about this high level of co-creating value. It's much more about the a little bit more specific steps that we have in the value chain that lead us to this value creation in the end. C says Service Management which are the specific organizational capabilities that we have as a service provider organization that we will utilize to continually co-create value with our stakeholders. D says the seven guiding principles which are guidances. They are a mindset and they are a way of how we could achieve continual co-creation of value with our customers, but the main purpose of co-creating value is within the service value system.

Question number 35 says value co-creation is done in which activity performed jointly by the service provider and service consumer organizations?

Value co-creation is done in which activity performed jointly by the Service Provider and Service Consumer organizations?

A. Service Delivery
B. Service Relationship Management
C. Service Consumption
D. Value Stream Mapping

The correct answer for this question would be B which says service relationship Management and that it is. Service relationship Management is all about having an understanding of who our stakeholders are and making sure that we can efficiently and effectively co-create value with them that we work together jointly. That's the key word in this question that we jointly perform activities between the service provider and the service consumer organizations, so it is service relationship Management. A says service delivery which is a one-sided activity coming from the service provider organization, which means we provide and we deliver services to our customers. C says service consumption which is the other end of this service delivery activity. They get the services. The customers consume the services that the service provider organization delivers so it's a one-sided activity. D says a value stream mapping which is just an exercise to understand how well you flow through the organization to understand which applications and services are involved in that and which teams are involved in that which allows us to create a more Agile organization.

Question number 36 says how does the knowledge Management practice support the improved service value chain activity?

How does the Knowledge Management practice support the *Improve* Service Value Chain activity?

A. By providing context for the assessment of achievements and improvement planning
B. By identifying specific CIs (Configuration Items) that often cause issues
C. By enabling new employees to easily access the knowledge most commonly used at the Service Desk
D. By allowing stakeholders to make informed decisions when it comes to the implementation of new strategies

The correct answer for this question would be A. A says by providing context for the assessment of achievements and improvement planning. Providing context means that whatever initiatives we had in the past or whatever improvements we wanted to achieve, knowledge Management ensures that the results and the conclusions are documented somewhere so these can be made available for use later on. For example when we are assessing our current achievements and we have a comparison to see how well we do compared to the previous achievements or the previous improvements that we had, which will also help us to create better plans for the future, because we have a context. We can say that we are doing better or worse compared to the last time we tried to improve or do something. B says by identifying specific configuration items that often cause issues. Not true because first of all that would be Problem Management and it would be in deliver and support. C says by enabling new employees to easily access the knowledge most commonly used at the Service Desk. While that is knowledge Management because we might have a cool knowledge base on a Service Desk where we have articles which can be easily used and linked with tickets, it would be done in the deliver and support service chain activity. D says by allowing stakeholders to make informed decisions when it comes to the implementation of new strategies. That's knowledge Management, however it's done in the plan service value chain activity and not within improve.

Question 37 says Governance, Management and communication is a consideration of which of the Service Management dimensions?

Governance, management, and communication is a consideration of which Service Management Dimension?

A. Value Streams and Processes
B. Partners and Suppliers
C. Organizations and People
D. Information and Technology

The correct answer for this would be C which says organizations and people and that is exactly it. We need to think about how to govern our organization and our people, how to make sure that our departments work together, how to control that they achieve their results, how to make sure that we don't have any bottlenecks and so on. We need to manage our organization and make sure that we have a good collaboration between different teams and the other parts of the organization, and it's also a lot about communication. I've seen that fail so often - the right communication methods and frequency and stakeholders are so important in modern organizations, so it's all about organizations and people. A says value streams and processes. While they also might need some level of governance and Management, it's mostly about understanding the flow of work and how we should achieve our goals. That's the purpose of value streams and processes. Partners and suppliers is all about understanding which partners we need and what our supplier strategy should look like and which partners to select and based on which Information to select them to make the decision on getting the right suppliers which fits our profile of our organization. D says Information and Technology which is all about making sure we have the right tools and right Information in place to make our services work as they are supposed to work so they can be seen as valuable by our customers and stakeholders. Governance, Management and communication is all about organization and people.

Question number 38 says which of the following is true for the Service Desk practice?

Which of the following is TRUE for the Service Desk practice?

A. It handles all Service Requests
B. Root cause analysis of Incidents happens here
C. It is important to have a high-level understanding of business processes
D. It connects stakeholders on strategic and tactical levels

The correct answer in this case would be C. It says it is important to have a high-level understanding of business processes and it is so true for the services practice. It's so good if we have a good understanding of how our business works because it will help us to troubleshoot much easier and much faster, because we get an understanding of what our customers do and how they work and how they utilize

181

our services and our products and our infrastructure. If we know on a high level how they work with those things that we provide, it might be much easier for us to find quick solutions for our customers and handle their Service Requests in a manner they would appreciate. A says it handles all Service Requests which is not true. While the Service Desk might handle a lot of Service Requests it's certainly not all as there might be special cases that need to be sent to second level teams or expert teams or other places of the organization. B says root cause analyzes of Incidents happens here. Not true because that is the Problem Management practice and while it might happen at the Service Desk, it is usually not the main job of the Service Desk. They might be involved, but it's mostly done at the expert teams because they have a higher chance of identifying recurring Incidents. D says it connects stakeholders on strategic and tactical levels. Not true. That is relationship Management practice because the Service Desk is much more about the operational level of the organization and not the strategic and tactical.

Question number 39 says ensuring normal service operation is the main goal of which practice?

Ensuring normal service operation is the main goal of which practice?

A. Problem Management
B. Incident Management
C. Service Desk
D. Service Level Management

The correct answer for this one would be B. It says Incident Management because that is the main goal of Incident Management. Make sure that whatever needs to work, works and that we put it back on the business track as soon as possible if something derailed, if something is not working, some issues are occurring we need to make sure that we provide the fastest possible solution to our customers ensuring that we reach our SLAs. Problem Management would be all about finding permanent solutions for recurring Incidents or for Incidents where we don't know what is causing them. If we have an unknown root cause that is all about Problem Management. C says the Service Desk which is kind of good answer and I might admit it might be a little bit confusing, but we should note that Service Desk is not only about Incident Management. It's not only about ensuring the normal service operation but it's also about Service Request Management and it might be about Problem Management or even Change Enablement because the Service Desk's main goal is to act as a main point of coordination or a single point of entry for our customers so they can reach the service provider organization if they need anything, and that might be Incidents or Service Requests, changes or problems and so on. D says service level Management which is not true because that is all about ensuring that we have service levels in place which have been agreed with our customers which are then enforced by the Incident Management practice for example but it's not about ensuring normal service operation. It's more about defining what normal service operation means according to our customers.

Question 40 says which practice provides Information of the organization's services by reporting on service performance?

Which practice provides information of the organization's services by reporting on service performance?

A. Monitoring and Event Management
B. Incident Management
C. Service Configuration Management
D. Service Level Management

That is a hard question but the correct one here would be D which is service level Management. Service level Management is all about defining the service levels with our customers, but it's also about reporting on those service levels that we have defined so if we said that I say something which could be a part of a service level, on a Service Desk 80 percent of all calls need to be taken within 20 seconds. That is an SLA, but then making sure that this SLA is reported to the customers in a service level report, that is done by the service level Management. They might delegate it to the services team leader for example but it's still the service level Management practice. A says monitoring and event Management which is all about detecting happenings in our infrastructure that could have effects on the organizational assets and on our services and making sure that we take the right actions based on the categorization of these events. B says Incident Management which is all about putting back the business train on track so ensuring normal service operation. C says service configuration Management which is more about understanding our configuration items which we have in our organization and how those config items connect with each other and how they relate to each other that we have a map of our infrastructure and services.

Questions number 41 says a set of organizational resources designed for performing work or accomplishing an objective is the definition of what?

"A set of organizational resources designed for performing work or accomplishing an objective" is the definition of what?

A. A process
B. A practice
C. A value stream
D. A service

The correct answer for this would be B. It is a practice or that's the definition of practices like Incident Management, Problem Management, Change Enablement and so on. These are organizational resources for performing work or accomplishing objectives because it's not only about the steps which are done in there. It's also about the people, it's about the Technology and it's about the Information that we need, the organization or the supplier so it's about all four dimensions and not only about the specific steps that need to be achieved because that would be processes. Those are specific steps which are needed to transform specific inputs into specific outputs. C says value streams which would be a series of steps that the organization undertakes to deliver valuable products to its customers. D says services which would be the means of enabling value co-creation to our customers without them having to take care of specific risks and specific costs which are involved in this value creation process.

Question number 42 says optimization should always start with which of the following?

Optimization should start with which of the following?

A. Having an understanding of the vision, mission and objectives of the organization
B. Ensuring that the management is aligned and on board
C. Securing financial funding
D. Standardizing procedures with a high potential for automatization

The correct answer for this question would be A which says; having an understanding of the vision mission and objectives of the organization. We can only optimize the right things if we understand what goals our organization has. We need to make sure that every improvement initiative, even the optimization of something should be aligned with whatever the organization wants to achieve because otherwise it would be a wasted effort. We need to make sure that we all pull the same strings or we row in the same direction and that's why it's important to understand the mission of the vision and objectives of our organization. B says ensuring that the Management is aligned and on board which is certainly not a bad thing but that's not the first thing to do. C says securing financial funding which is certainly necessary but if we align first with the vision of the mission and objectives of our organization securing financial funding should not be a problem. So that's not the first thing. D says standardizing procedures with a high potential for automatization, which is a very good thing because even the guiding principle says optimize and automate but before we start optimization we should have the vision and mission understanding and only then once the optimization has been done, we can start thinking about standardizing and automatizing things.

Question number 43 says which of the following practices may initiate disaster recovery procedures?

Which of the following practices may initiate disaster recovery procedures?

A. Service Request Management
B. Service Level Management
C. Change Enablement
D. Incident Management

The correct answer in this case would be D which says Incident Management. Here we are specifically talking about major Incidents because they might very well initiate disaster recovery procedures and steps because if something is failing really hard, then we should go for disaster recovery procedures, even to evacuate people from the building if something hits that hard, but usually it's not the case. Usually we are talking about IT Incidents like a server is failing or maybe we have a key application or core application within our organization and for some reason there is an Incident in the data center and we cannot somehow resolve it quickly and in that case we might switch to another data center which is very well a disaster recovery procedure. A says Service Request Management which has nothing to do with disasters because it's only about customers and people in the organization want to have some additional stuff or some new stuff like new monitors or access rights so no disaster recovery get there. Service level Management is all about having the right SLAs in place and making sure that we understand what our customers need in these terms and they might be even talking about disaster recovery steps and when to initiate disaster recovery procedures, but it's not about initiating those because it's Incident Management. Change Enablement is making sure that we are having the right controls in place to make sure that the right authorities need to approve the changes which are need to be pushed into the productive environment but there is usually no disaster recovery procedures involved in this. Even if a change fails very hard, we have a backup plan to restore the previous state of the service but that's not disaster recovery in this sense.

Question number 44 says how does the relationship Management practice support the engaged service value chain activity?

How does the Relationship Management practice support the *Engage* Service Value Chain activity?

A. It ensures that all Incidents are solved within the defined SLAs
B. By making sure that all stakeholders are involved into planning activities
C. By ensuring high levels of customer satisfaction in the handling of Incidents and Service Requests
D. It is responsible for engaging with all internal an external customers to understand their requirements

The correct answer in this case is D which says, it is responsible for engaging with all internal and external customers to understand their requirements. Relationship Management is anyway a lot about engagement, understanding our stakeholders needs and talk to them make sure we understand what they want, how they feel about our services and our products and make sure that we have an understanding of what they need. We gather and we try to understand their requirements so D is the correct answer. A says it ensures that all Incidents are solved within the defined SLAs. Not true. That would be Incident Management and it would be in deliverance support. B says by making sure that all stakeholders are involved into planning activities and while it is relationship Management, it is done in a plan service value chain activity. C says by ensuring high levels of customer satisfaction in the handling of Incident and Service Request. While it might be a mix of relationship Management doing that, maybe even service level Management and the Incident Management practice and the service desk practice but it's not happening in the engaged service value chain activity. It's happening in the um deliver and support service by a chain activity.

Question number 45 says what is a missing word? A known error is a problem that has been... and has not been resolved.

What is the missing word?

A known error is a problem that has been _____ and has not been resolved.

A. Analyzed
B. Documented
C. Identified
D. Escalated

The correct answer in this case would be A which says analyze and that is true. A known error is a problem that has already been analyzed but it is not solved yet because we cannot call it a problem anymore. The problem is the unknown cause of one or more Incidents and once we know the cause because we have analyzed it, we call it a known error and then we try to solve that to make sure that the permanent solution is in place, making sure it's never happening again. B says documented. Not true because once we document the problem it's still called a problem. C says identified. Well if once it's identified it's called the problem again and just because we escalate it like said in D, it doesn't change anything about the fact. So a problem is still a problem even if it's escalated to another support team, even though most of the times the Problem Management practice is a very parallel practice - meaning that a lot of teams are involved the in the solution of this problem and into the analysis of the problem at the same time.

Question number 46 says the Service Request Management practice relies on what for maximum efficiency?

The Service Request Management practice relies on what for maximum efficiency?

A. Processes and Procedures
B. The Service Desk
C. Service Level Agreements
D. Self-Service tools and web shops

The correct answer for this would be A which says processes and procedures. We need to make sure that the Service Request handling first of all automated as much as possible to save some time especially on the services but maybe also another support teams, but it's also important to have a clear understanding of how specific Service Requests need to be handled. If somebody wants to have a new password, how is it done? If somebody is ordering a new standard application, how is it done? If somebody has a completely new requirement for the organization, how is it done? We need to document these processes and procedures into so-called Service Request models and then those would very much help us to efficiently solve and finish those Service Requests. B says the Service Desk and while it's true because the request Management practice certainly relies on a Service Desk it's not only about the Service Desk. Service Requests might very well be handled at other support teams as well. C says service level agreements and while the Service Request handling might be part of the SLA where we say how much time we have for the handling of different Service Requests, it's very often not the case that we include them in the SLAs, but they are still counting as normal service Operations, so officially they should be in there. We should have a service catalog for our Service Requests which defines what counts as standard and what doesn't count as standard services. D says self-service tools and web shops which are certainly a very nice addition to have like cool portals where your customers could log in and they can just order something which makes it highly automatable where we can make sure that somebody orders let's see an access right to an application and then it's automatically going to the right approval person, and then it's automatically deployed once the approval has taken place with nobody involved in it. But officially it's more about the processes and procedures than about the actual tools and Technology behind it.

Question number 47 says every problem ticket should have what or should be what?

Every Problem ticket...

A. Should have a workaround to reduce the impact
B. Should be resolved so it can be closed quickly
C. Should be diagnosed to identify solutions
D. Should be prioritized based on probability an impact

The correct answer for this one would be D. It says all the problems should be prioritized based on the probability of occurrence and the impact on the organization and that is true. That needs to be done for every single problem ticket. Doesn't matter how many problems we have but it needs to be done because it will help us to identify which problems to tackle first and to create an order which to handle because Problem Management is kind of time intensive. It can consume a lot of time and a lot of resources in different teams so we need to make sure that we really handle the problems with the highest priority first. A says all the problems should have a workaround to reduce the impact. While this is nice to have it's certainly not a must because there will be problems which do not have workarounds in place and this is a hard pill to swallow but it might be really the case so not all problems can have a workaround. B says all the problems should be resolved so they can be closed quickly. Not true. It could be nice to have again but it's not a must because there will be problems we will not touch because they are simply not important to be handled especially not quickly because the time factor is more in the Incident Management practice where we need to handle things ASAP. C says they should be diagnosed to identify solutions. Again, it should be done but maybe not for every problem ticket. There might be problems which are more important than the others and it might very well be that smaller problems which maybe don't affect a lot of people or maybe they don't have a huge impact or maybe they have a good workaround are never handled.

Question number 48 says how does the supplier Management practice support the obtain build service value chain activity?

How does the Supplier Management practice support the *Obtain/Build* Service Value Chain activity?

A. By ensuring that the vendor selection procedure is based on the culture of the service provider organization
B. By supporting the procurement of services or components from third parties
C. By acting as a single point of contact (SPOC) for the Service Desk when vendor support is needed
D. By providing the organization's sourcing strategy

The correct one for this would be B which says by supporting the procurement of services or components from third parties. Third parties are our vendors and our suppliers and when it comes to obtain and build value service chain activity, it's all about first of all deciding if we should buy something or build something and then get that stuff. So if we decided that something should be bought from a vendor or a third party, then it would be supplier Management practice which helps with the support of getting those components. A says by ensuring that a vendor selection procedure is based on the culture of the service provider organization. While this is an important point and it should happen and it is done by the supplier Management practice, but it is done in the engaged service value chain activity. C says by acting as a single point of contact for the Service Desk when vendor support is needed. Well, triggering this would be done by the Incident Management practice when we need the vendors and it might be the case that we have a special team for doing this, that is called CIAM or service integration and Management and some organizations might have it but it's not in the obtain and build. It would much more be in the deliver and support value chain activity if we have something like this. D says by providing the organization sourcing strategy and while supplier Management does that it does it in the plan service value chain activity.

Question number 49 says how to best define what an output is?

How to best define what an Output is?

A. An event of unknown effect to the organization
B. The first, potentially usable increment of work done
C. Something that is created as the result of an activity
D. A valuable result for one or more stakeholders

The correct answer for this question would be C which says an output is something that is created as the result of an activity. We do something, we have a process or some procedure or some activities and what is created based on that or as a result of that activity, that would be an outcome. A says an event of unknown effect to the organization which would be a risk. Could be positive like an opportunity or negative like a hazard but it's still a risk. B says the first potentially usable increment of work which is done, that would be a minimum viable product an MVP as known from the different Agile ways of working and D says a valuable result for one or more stakeholders, but that would be an outcome. We might have multiple outputs which feed into outcomes but still an outcome is the result of an activity like said in C.

We have arrived at our last question - question number 50 which says what is the benefit of the services stuff identifying recurring issues?

What is the benefit of the Service Desk staff identifying recurring issues?

A. It helps to identify Problems
B. It helps to keep the agreed SLAs
C. It increases customer satisfaction
D. It helps to escalate tickets to the correct expert team

The correct answer one for this one is A. It says it helps to identify problems. Exactly! Recurring issues should result in the creation of problem tickets because that's the definition of problems. The unknown cause of one or more Incidents or maybe recurring Incidents - that's always a problem. So if the service says stuff identifies that there are issues and the same issues happening over and over and over again, they should trigger the creation of a problem ticket and maybe they do it themselves or maybe they just inform the second level team who is responsible for that but technically they could do it themselves and then the Problem Management practice would be initiated. B says it helps to keep the agreed SLAs. Well, not really true in the end because just because we know that something is happening over and over again, it might lead to resolving the Incidents with the comment that there is a problem take it open for it but still it's not the main purpose or it's not the main benefit. C says it increases customer satisfaction and that might be true if we resolve all these recurring issues, customers might be happier but not necessarily so it's much more about A identifying problems then increasing customer satisfaction. D says it helps to escalate tickets to the correct expert team. Certainly not true because just because we know it's recurring we don't know which team we need to escalate it to. There is no straight correlation between these two pieces of Information, so the correct answer here is A.

Conclusion

Congratulations on completing this book! I am sure you have plenty on your belt, but please don't forget to leave an honest review on Amazon. Furthermore, if you think this information was helpful to you, please share anyone who you think would be interested of IT as well.

About Richie Miller

Richie Miller has always loved teaching people Technology. He graduated with a degree in radio production with a minor in theatre in order to be a better communicator. While teaching at the Miami Radio and Television Broadcasting Academy, Richie was able to do voiceover work at a technical training company specializing in live online classes in Microsoft, Cisco, and CompTia technologies. Over the years, he became one of the top virtual instructors at several training companies, while also speaking at many tech and training conferences. Richie specializes in Project Management and ITIL these days, while also doing his best to be a good husband and father.

www.ingramcontent.com/pod-product-compliance
Lightning Source LLC
Chambersburg PA
CBHW071118050326
40690CB00008B/1263